A GARDEN
FOR ALL
SEASONS

A GARDEN
FOR ALL
SEASONS

STEFAN BUCZACKI

CONRAN OCTOPUS

First published in 1990 by
Conran Octopus Limited,
37 Shelton Street,
London WC2H 9HN

British Library Cataloguing in Publication Data
Buczacki, Stefan T, 1945–
    A garden for all seasons.
    1. Gardening
    I. Title
    635

    ISBN 1-85029-235-3

         Project Editor   Cortina Butler
            Art Editor   Helen Lewis
     Picture Research   Jessica Walton
           Production   Jackie Kernaghan
          Copy Editor   Mary Trewby
   Editorial Assistant   Denise Bates
            Designer   Mike Snell
         Illustrations   Nancy Anderson
                        Vanessa Luff

Typeset by Bookworm Typesetting, Manchester
Printed and bound in Hong Kong

CONTENTS

Introduction

Few leisure pursuits are so inextricably tied to the changing seasons as is gardening. But whilst some people go out of their way to ensure that something keeps them occupied for all twelve months of the year, for others it is an activity for one season alone. Whether you fall into one of these categories or, like the majority, take a median view, there is no denying that to garden successfully, you must be in tune with Nature's activities.

Over the years, there have been several books listing, month by month, the tasks to be performed in the garden. And pretty uninspired reading they make. This in itself depresses me for gardening is a pursuit so full of interest, excitement and reward that to reduce it to bare lists is to do it a serious disservice. This book is different; different because although I have given you many tasks to follow, I have also tried to convey something of the pleasure that gardens and gardening give to me; but different most importantly because I have described the ways in which the seasons themselves dictate our activities. For gardening, I believe, is merely Nature under a modest amount of control. We cannot decide when our seeds will germinate or the apples ripen, when the shrubs should be pruned or the weeds be hoed. The timing of these things is dependent on Nature's choice but it helps us to plan our activities if we understand some of the principles that govern them.

Most of us are enthralled by natural history documentaries on television yet there are stories and events just as fascinating, just as dramatic, taking place in every garden, be it urban or rural, tiny or vast. Beneath every leaf there is life, hiding from the sun and the rain; beneath every stone, there is a miniature jungle, a struggle for existence between competing natural organisms. By appreciating why

An understanding of the fascinating processes at work in a garden will enhance enjoyment of its changing character throughout the year. Every season has its own particular charms, from the obvious and colourful delights of spring and summer through to the stark and misty landscapes of winter.

these creatures live in our gardens, which of them work to our benefit and which against it, and how they are affected by changing temperatures, changing soil moisture, wind or day length, we can plan our actions or reactions most meaningfully. And if we know *how* plants grow and mature, we shall understand better *why* they must be fed at certain times and pruned at others, or lifted and divided in one season but left alone in another.

For each of the four seasons therefore, I begin with an account of the garden's own activities, the facets of plant and animal life that give each period of the year its own special character. The seasonal tasks will then seem more logical and easy to understand. And to render them simple to follow, I have grouped the tasks under a number of categories – flowers, vegetables, greenhouse and so forth. In my descriptions of tasks, I have divided each season into early, middle and late without attempting precisely to name individual months. This is simply because, through attempting precision, I could merely mislead for the weather and climate can vary markedly in a single month even within a fairly small geographical region. Such signposts as the date of the last frost are much more valuable indicators.

So, this book is about performing the routine tasks of gardening through understanding. But it is also a book about looking ahead, being forearmed with knowledge and information in order to plan for the next and subsequent seasons. I have approached the subject of planning by inviting you to look at the various features of gardens as they reach their peak; and then to explain at which other times you will need to make certain decisions or perform particular tasks in order to achieve the desired effect.

Gardening has never failed to give me both satisfaction and inspiration. And over the years, both have increased as my understanding of gardening has advanced. I hope that this book will take you along the same path; and if it results in your deriving only a fraction of the pleasure from gardening that I have experienced, I shall have amply succeeded.

7

SPRING

The first warm breeze of spring encourages the gardener to linger outdoors and delight in the glory of the spring flowers. Contrasting with the muted tones of winter, the blue of ceanothus (left) or bluebells, the yellow of primroses, daffodils or potentilla (far left) and the red of tulips, all complemented by the clear green of freshly unfurled leaves, illuminate the garden with brilliant patches of colour.

SPRING NOTES

A Time of Reproduction

The mere thought of spring seems to stir the soul. Wherever you look in the garden at this time of year, brown twigs are turning green, bare earth is yielding up succulent new shoots and the early season's flowers are slowly signalling the brightness and warm encouragement of another gardening summer. Spring is the season of life, when so many types of plants and animals, quite literally, go forth and multiply.

In reality, much of our gardening endeavour is directed towards encouraging plants to reproduce themselves. Although foliage, either for ornamental appeal or eating, is certainly the reason for cultivating

Bright spring flowers such as *Anemone blanda* (*above*), fritillaries and speedwell (*centre*), and primroses (*above right*), often look appealing if planted in a semi-wild, partially shaded part of the garden and allowed to naturalize.

many types of garden plants, its importance in most gardens is outweighed by that of flowers and fruits (both edible or ornamental).

In botanical terms, a flower is merely a structure in which a female ovule is fertilized by male pollen as a prelude to the formation of seeds, perhaps contained in a fruit, and hence the continuation of the species. But we never seem satisfied with what Nature has provided. Natural flowers are seldom good enough for us and, over the years, gardeners and plant breeders have sought to change them (or improve them, to use a favourite nineteenth-century expression). For reasons that are not always understandable, there is a general preference for bigger flowers, double flowers, and flowers in colours different from those that occur naturally. But in achieving these objectives – by repeated cross breeding and selections – there is a good chance of removing the flowers' basic functional features. Flowers (at least, most of the ornamental flowers of garden plants) are supposed to attract insects. When altered, they may be changed to a colour that insects find less appealing, the perfume that insects adore may be bred out of them and, most importantly, in producing double flowers, the stamens might be converted into more petals. And so, no stamens, no pollen, no seeds, and no more plants.

Therefore, having produced the double flowers so beloved of rose,

dahlia, chrysanthemum and other flower gardeners, we should be grateful for all the succulent green shoots and the unseen vigour stirring in roots below ground. These provide plants with quite a different method of multiplication from pollination: it is called vegetative reproduction. Divisions and cuttings of small, non-flowering parts of a plant which are separated from the parent and then planted in soil or compost, in due course, form new roots. Generally, it is spring that is the best time for propagating them. This is when sap is rising and tissues are growing vigorously, so producing the hormones necessary for regeneration to proceed rapidly.

The mass of blossom weighing down the branches in an apple orchard will attract insects to pollinate these and other flowers in the garden.

How Temperature Affects Growth

I can think of no living things that, when slightly below par, do not benefit from being given 'a little extra warmth'. It is something that we take for granted with children, old people, pets and of course plants – warmth is life giving and growth enhancing. And in spring, as temperatures rise all around us, the mere thought of increased warmth is enough to shrug off winter's gloom. But the relationship between living things and temperature isn't quite as straightforward as it might appear at first sight.

All growth depends on chemical changes that take place within the cells of living organisms, whether they be humans, other animals or plants: they are all dependent on very similar chemical reactions. When the temperature rises or falls, the chemical reactions are speeded up or slowed down. And, curiously, although plants and animals have colonized and adapted to life on all parts of the planet, their growth rates vary by very little. The optimum temperature for all living organisms is between about 10°C and 25°C (50°F and 77°F); they grow little below 5°C (41°F) and above 30°C (86°F). In other words, plants growing in consistently very hot or very cold regions (cacti and alpines, for example) tend to grow very slowly. The quickest growing plants are species of the tropical rain forest where the temperature is never extreme – a range between 22°C and 32°C (72°F and 90°F) is fairly normal – and, of course, there is constant moisture and plenty of nutrients to help them grow.

At one time in their lives, however, almost all plants require – or, at least, appreciably benefit from – a slightly higher temperature than they ever require again. This is to promote seed germination and, although the need for the higher temperature is sometimes associated with the breaking of dormancy-inducing mechanisms (see below), it is also a general feature of the stirring into action of juvenile tissue. The value of this is most noticeable in the spring garden when cloches or even sheets of plastic have been used to pre-warm the soil before sowing seeds outdoors: not only do the seeds germinate more rapidly but they do so more uniformly. And, generally, a greater number of seeds will germinate successfully: the longer an ungerminated seed lies in the soil, the more likely it is that the seed will be attacked by insects, other pests or decay-causing fungi and bacteria.

Emerging from Dormancy

Too frequently, gardeners forget that plants actually have a life (as their ancestors did before them) beyond the garden boundaries. They are natural, wild things and many of them originate in climates rather more extreme than our own. Imagine a plant from a cool temperate climate producing its flowers in the early summer, being pollinated and then setting its seeds as autumn approaches. The seeds are shed on to the soil or perhaps dispersed by wind or other carrier to locations some distance from the parent. The soil in autumn may well be warm and moist and full of nutrients – in effect, no different from its condition in the spring. But the future for the seeds would be very different indeed: for seeds germinating in the spring, temperatures are rising gradually and growing conditions are ideal; a seedling that emerges in the autumn would have to face temperatures that are falling, and eventually frosts which would lay low its tender young tissues.

The candelabra primulas and hostas that grow beside this woodland stream have lain dormant through the winter only to emerge as the days lengthen and the temperature of the air and soil rises.

The danger for seedlings of plants from hot regions of the world – where frost is unknown but where the rainfall tends to be more seasonal – is in emerging at a time when, although the soil is moist and the weather warm, the rainy season is ending and the temperature rising to damagingly high levels. For the plants as species to survive, the individual seedlings must be protected against such inhospitable conditions: this is the reason many seeds have an inbuilt mechanism – the sleeping state, or dormancy as it is more correctly known – that ensures they only germinate when the environmental conditions are suitable for the young plants to grow and survive.

This inbuilt mechanism may take several forms, most of which involve the presence in the seed coat of chemicals that suppress the seed's ability to germinate. Sometimes these chemicals are diluted to an ineffective level when the seeds are subjected to prolonged and heavy rainfall. Yet others among the chemical suppressors are inactivated by periods of high temperature, so mimicking a natural hot summer before the onset of a rainy season. But in most garden plant seeds, the suppressors are rendered ineffective when exposed to prolonged cold temperature: they will benefit if you imitate the effects of winter by keeping the seeds in the refrigerator for two or three weeks.

Struggling for Life

Although it may often appear that in a garden it is we, the gardeners, who struggle most of all, there is a whole series of miniature wars taking place around us. In spring, every time we sow a seed or plant a plant, we are subjecting the individual to a competition in which the prize for winning is life and the penalty for losing is a gradual decline into oblivion. It is a competition for food, water and space – space for roots to grow through the soil, and space above ground for leaves and shoots to reach the sunlight. And the competing plants may belong to different species or be members of the same species; the garden in spring provides graphic examples of both.

The most obvious competition between different types of plants takes place when the native vegetation appears in beds and borders in the guise of weeds (see page 20). But there is rivalry too between the many different types of plants in a mixed or herbaceous border. The skill in making such a border comes from knowing the colours, textures and flowering times of different types of flowers, and then blending them together in a way that creates the maximum effect for the longest possible time. But the different heights and spreads of the chosen varieties should also be taken into account so that the natural competitiveness of the plants does not take over. For instance, there is no merit in planting a small, slow-growing species such as a saxifrage just in front of a vigorous, spreading herbaceous geranium such as 'Claridge Druce'. The colour blend may be perfect, the flowering times complementary but the saxifrage will never achieve its potential because of its overpowering companion.

Least appreciated is the rivalry between different plants of the same type. Yet, in spring, when new seeds are being sown weekly and new seedlings emerging all the time, this type of competition is critical, particularly for the success of vegetable gardens. On every seed packet there are some instructions that have a bearing on this competition: for example, the distances apart at which the seeds should be placed, or the

In a border closely planted with a mixture of shrubs, perennials and bulbs, every element is competing for light and nutrients, but if plants with different heights and growth habits are selected and the ground is kept well fertilized, each has the maximum opportunity to flourish.

distances between young seedlings that have been thinned or singled. These measurements are those that are supposed to limit the competition between individual plants so that they do not affect each other's yield adversely, and yet still allow the optimum overall yield to be obtained from the available growing area. In practice, the traditional spacing distances may not be the best, for many of them position plants too close together within each row (so they compete with each other) and leave large gaps that weeds are able to colonize between the rows. With many vegetable crops, for instance, broad beans (see Spring Tasks 59), competition is minimized and yield enhanced by spacing the plants equidistantly, in blocks rather than rows.

Rotating Crops

'A change is as good as a rest' is not a bad maxim for a great many aspects of life. It has its gardening significance too, a significance that becomes apparent as the new season's vegetable crop begins to grow and mature. For almost without exception, vegetables grow and yield better if they are not planted where the same type of vegetables grew the year before. What a curious state of affairs this is, for if you take almost any natural or semi-natural habitat – a wood, meadow, stream bank or cliff top for instance – the same plants, or at least the same types of plants, thrive in more or less the same places for year after year. How can Nature succeed when we as gardeners cannot?

In the final analysis, I suppose it could be said to come down to greed and dissatisfaction. Or it could be expressed in terms of wanting the very best return for your efforts. If you compare the plants grown in the vegetable garden with their wild ancestors, the differences are usually so great that the relationship is barely recognizable. The tiny, slender pod of the wild vetch would look much less appealing on the plate than the plump succulent garden pea picked from your own garden. Two of the principal reasons for the difference are embodied in the practice of crop rotation: first, the wild plants are very probably living in a delicate balance with pests and diseases, which can suppress their vigour generally; and, second, the wild plants are wholly reliant for their food on such nutrients as come their way, through fallen leaves and other plant debris, and hence through natural humus.

By moving or rotating vegetables, year by year, the impact of pests and diseases can be diminished to some extent. Many of the problems that live in the soil, such as root-attacking maggots and root-rotting fungi, are rather specific in respect of the types of plants they attack and thrive on: if their favoured crops are not grown on a particular area of soil for three years or so, they may be expected to die away and, therefore, when the original types of plants return, the soil should present a healthy environment once again.

The nutritional benefits of crop rotation derive from the fact that each type of plant requires slightly differing amounts of the major nutrients and, usually, a slightly different range of the minor ones. By rotating the types of plants grown on a particular area of soil each year, the natural spectrum of nutrients in the soil is utilized to the full.

Of course, both the presence of pests and diseases and the nutrients in gardens are also affected very significantly by the use of direct pest- and disease-control measures and of fertilizers. But crop rotation is a most important adjunct to both these practices.

As the warmth of the spring sun stimulates growth in the vegetable garden, the benefits of crop rotation become apparent. Only by moving the planting position of vegetables every year will a good yield from the plot be sustained.

The Green, Green Grass

Invariably, at the precise moment when your gardening hands are most completely occupied – when the greenhouse bulges with seed trays that seem to turn ever more lush by the hour, when the cold frame appears to shrink before your eyes as more and more tender young things are moved into it for hardening off, and the first signs of mildew can be seen on the rose bushes – you realize that the great green monster has stirred into life again. We call this monster a lawn, and its renewed vigour is the surest of signs that spring has sprung.

Having a lawn is a relatively easy way of keeping an extensive area of plant life under control. And such a uniform area of green provides an

A swathe has been cut through a field of long grass and moon daisies (*above*) but neither this, nor the mowing to which a neat garden lawn (*right*) is subjected, will stop grass from growing, although it would be fatal to most other plants.

excellent foil to other, less restrained, plantings in the garden: it 'sets off' the beds, borders, trees and shrubs.

Most lawns are made of grass. The quality that sets it apart from the tens of thousands of other types of plants is, quite simply, that grass can be mown. Grasses are unusual in that they grow from the bottom upwards. The special tissues that elongate the shoots are at ground level, not at the tips as they are in most others: if you cut the top off a lettuce it will die because it cannot produce any more leaves, but if you shave the top off grass, it will grow again perfectly happily (see page 48). Of course, grasses have not evolved in this way simply so that we can mow them, but to enable them to continue growing even when

repeatedly grazed by animals. Our gardening forebears used scythes to produce a relatively even grass surface. It was certainly not the smooth, velvety turf around country houses seen in films set in the eighteenth century. Such billiard-table perfection only came after 1830 when a gentleman called Buddin invented the cylinder lawn mower by adapting a machine used for taking the nap off cloth.

If you share the modern fondness for native plants in the garden and have sown or planted a 'wild flower meadow', do remember that many of the component plants will die once they are mown. As many of them are annuals, it is important to wait until late in the summer before taking the rotary mower to your 'meadow'. By then, the seeds will have matured and if you leave the mowings for a while to dry, as farmers do with hay, seeds will be shed to give you more wild flowers next year.

More difficult to manage are the non-grass lawns, made of thyme or chamomile, for instance. These are plants that have an ability to regenerate from basal buds or – like many common lawn weeds, such as dandelions and daisies – have their growth points sunk down on the tips of very abbreviated shoots. They produce a lawn that will not withstand being walked on to any great extent, that looks dismal in winter and, because it is impossible to use selective weedkillers on it, can quickly become unsightly.

The Noble Weeds

I have grown weary of the definition of a weed as 'a plant growing in the wrong place'. I much prefer the view that a weed is 'a plant whose potential has not yet been recognized'. But whatever we may think of them, it is impossible to ignore weeds, particularly in the spring when they are becoming more and more prominent wherever we look in the garden. The soil that appeared so fresh and brown when the beds were forked over sprouts a miniature forest within a few weeks.

But we should appreciate that weeds are simply the native vegetation attempting to reclaim their ground from the alien hordes that have been deposited in their midst. And because weeds *are* native plants, they are the ones that generally succeed if we don't intervene. After all, they have had thousands of years to adapt to the local environmental conditions. They will win against garden plants for all manner of reasons: perhaps because they grow more rapidly or more extensively, or because they produce multitudes of seeds that result in armies of seedlings swamping beds and borders through force of numbers.

Of the several hundred types of plants that can crop up in the guise of weeds, perhaps 50 are of importance in any one area; these can be divided into three important categories: annuals, deep-rooted perennials and lawn weeds.

Annuals are the fast growers and fast reproducers. Like annual bedding plants, their life cycle spans a single season during which time the seeds germinate and the seedlings grow to maturity, flower and, in turn, set seeds of their own. Some seeds must lie over winter in the soil before they can germinate; others, lacking any dormancy mechanism, can germinate almost immediately and, in a few instances, actually pass through more than one generation in a year. It is not difficult to control annual weeds: the key is to ensure that they are destroyed before their seeds have been set. In beds, borders and other areas that are disturbed relatively infrequently, the simplest method of control is by mulching. A

Bulbous plants allowed to naturalize, such as fritillaries and daffodils, should not be cut back immediately after they have flowered otherwise their underground food stores will not be replenished. It is sometimes a good idea therefore to plant them in a part of the garden which does not require regular mowing.

layer of organic mulch, approximately 5 cm (2 in) thick, suppresses almost all annual weed growth by starving their seedlings of light. In the vegetable garden and other areas where a more or less permanent cover of mulch is impracticable, weeds can be controlled by using the Dutch or similar hoe to sever their stems; however, do this during dry weather or the result will be weed transplantation rather than control.

Deep-rooted or far-creeping perennial weeds can be dug out physically in some circumstances: the area must be free of other plants and the soil must be easily workable. In a heavy clay or where existing

plants obstruct progress, fragments of root or rhizome can break away easily and regenerate, multiplying the original. In these conditions, the only reliable control measure is to use translocated weedkiller which is taken up by the plant and carried down to reach the hidden parts.

Lawn weeds were once the bane of all gardeners, who were limited to daisy grubbing tools in the battle to remove them. Today the problem is simply one of choosing the optimum time to apply a selective lawn weedkiller: when the soil is warm and moist and both weeds and grass are growing vigorously. I hesitate to say that modern weedkillers have taken away all of the anguish that spring brings to the garden, but they do help you to concentrate on the more endearing tasks of the season.

PLANNING THE SPRING GARDEN

After the dark tones of winter, bulbs bring a sudden burst of invigorating spring colour into the garden (*above*). Red tulips blaze amongst green foliage and against the dark background of a yew hedge. In early summer, when the tulips have died down and been transplanted, the pastel shades of lupins (*right*) take over.

An Abundance of Bulbs

Spring has really arrived when the first bulbs flower. These early season blooms should be merely the beginning of a long succession of flowering bulbs (and I include among the group those that, strictly speaking, form not bulbs but corms or tubers instead) that lasts through summer and beyond. Most good garden centres now stock a wide range of bulbs, including numerous varieties of old favourites such as daffodils, crocuses and tulips as well as an increasing number of less familiar species (alliums, chionodoxas, leucojums and ornithogalums, for instance). But versatile though bulbs are, they will not grow just anywhere. The secrets of success are to choose the correct types for each garden situation and to select species and varieties carefully in order to give the maximum impact. Fortunately, most modern bulb packets give useful details of size, flowering time and specific site requirements.

Bulbs may be planted formally or informally, in beds with other spring flowers, in borders for blending with herbaceous perennials later in the season, beneath trees, in rock gardens, in established grass (although preferably not in mown lawns where they interfere with the mowing operations), in containers, or tucked away in odd and difficult corners. But there are some overall, general guidelines applicable to most situations.

Wherever bulbs are to be planted, they must have good, well-drained soil because their soft fleshy structure is highly prone to the activity of decay organisms. This is especially important if you plan to plant them into established grass. In this situation lifting the turf and lightening the soil with very thoroughly rotted compost or manure well in advance repays good dividends. You should *never* use fresh manure for bulbs.

Most types of bulbs can be allowed to naturalize – in other words, they do not require lifting after they have flowered – but there are a few exceptions, and such bulbs should not be planted where their annual removal will interfere with other types of plant. The few half-hardy types such as gladioli, together with large-

flowered tulips, are the most important of these. Although perfectly hardy, the tulips are somewhat prone to attack by insects and other types of pest when left in the ground over winter; however, their foliage must be left until it has completely yellowed (the leaves can be cut from other types of bulb six weeks after the flowers have faded). So, if large-flowered tulips are planted – as they generally are – in positions that are to be occupied by other types of plant during the summer, they must be lifted and *transplanted* temporarily (into the vegetable plot, for instance) after flowering, to be left until the foliage has completely died down. Do be sure that you have an area of ground of adequate size available for this purpose.

Daffodils look their best when planted in swathes and left to naturalize in a semi-wild environment. They seem to find their natural focus when clustered around a tree.

Pale-coloured flowers really need a dark backdrop if their colour is to be truly appreciated. These pale pink tulips are offset by the weathered brick wall behind but they would look equally effective against a tree trunk or bank of dark foliage. In a border such as this it is particularly important to plant the bulbs close together, to avoid any danger of a bare appearance when the flowers emerge.

Very pale bulbs such as white snowdrops and the many yellow-flowered types always look at their best when planted against a darker background. With snowdrops, in bloom when deciduous plants are still hibernating, this background must be provided by an evergreen plant or some structural feature of the garden – a wall or the base of a tree trunk, for instance. (On the subject of bulbs beneath trees, the rapidly spreading, shade-tolerant types such as snowdrops or cyclamen are valuable as ground cover for the early and late parts of the season.)

Even within the same type of bulbous plant there may be a wide range of colours available. But, if the plants are bought as mixed varieties, there can be bizarre and jarring colour clashes. Although this might not matter with, say, hybrid tulips which will be removed after the season, it can be a long-term irritation with permanently planted forms, such as large-flowered Dutch crocuses; for example, the combination of orange, purple and white would not look as effective as keeping the purple and white together and orange separate. So I strongly advise buying bulbs as individual named varieties rather than the mixtures often offered by suppliers.

Daffodils (*left*) can be successful in the slightly more formal setting of a border. Try interplanting discrete groups of different varieties, such as the large-trumpeted 'Golden Harvest' and, for contrast, a delicate, white-flowered narcissus.

Not only do tulips and forget-me-nots (*below*) create a lovely contrast in colour and stature, but in practical terms it makes sense to interplant tulips with an early-flowering annual so that both can be lifted together to make way for the summer bedding plants.

Buying separately has the advantage, too, that you can choose varieties with staggered flowering times. Planted in groups of about ten individuals (as with daffodils and narcissi, where the golden types tend to be earlier than the white forms), these give continuity of bloom. And planting close together in groups means that the later types will not have to push their way through the dead flower heads of their predecessors, as happens when they are all jumbled together. Even when bulbs are planted formally in beds (and it is only the large-flowered tulips that really look effective or like this type

of planting), placing them wide apart in rows creates a pathetic appearance. Close planting – say, 8 cm (3 in) apart and slightly off-set from their neighbours – is much more appropriate. The food reserve in the bulb ensures that the plants do not suffer from the competition; giving them liquid fertilizer after flowering builds up their strength again. In practice, interplanting tulips with early-flowering annuals, such as forget-me-nots, or with biennial wallflowers makes good sense for they can all be taken up at the same time to make space for summer-flowering hardy and half-hardy annuals.

Bulbs, like most other types of plants, grow well in containers. The best bulbs to plant are those with strongly scented flowers such as hyacinths and some of the lilies for the containers may be placed close to a door or pathway where the perfume can be most enjoyed. To obtain continuity of flowering within the confined space of a container, plant two varieties, one flowering later than the other, at two separate depths: if the later-flowering bulbs are placed about 7 cm (2¾ in) deeper and between the earlier ones, they will emerge just as the dead heads are being snipped from the first blooms.

Steps to a Perfect Lawn

Far too frequently I hear gardeners complain about the weekly (or, preferably, twice-weekly) task of lawn mowing. I always respond by reminding them of how much greater a chore they would find tending the same area of ground if it were cultivated in some other way. Another quite different factor, too, sets a lawn apart from other ways of covering the same expanse. Gravel and paving certainly have their uses in the garden, concrete has a very minor role (and tarmac none at all), but over a large area these surfaces never look as effective as grass.

Laying a lawn is also a good solution for the person moving to a new garden who wishes to take time to plan. It is very easy to remove areas of the grass at a later date when the layout of other features has been decided upon. And in the interim, of course, regular mowing will keep weed growth well under control.

In an ideal world, the ground for a new lawn should be dug and prepared by incorporating organic matter in advance, much as it is for other types of plants. In practice, the size of the area involved usually makes this degree of thoroughness impracticable; nonetheless, especially on a virgin site, it is well worth using a rotary cultivator both to turn over the soil and then to break it down into a finer tilth. But before taking cultivator, spade or fork to the area, it is wise to spray the whole with glyphosate, the translocated total weedkiller: although it is perfectly possible to eradicate perennial broad-leaved weeds later by using a selective lawn weedkiller (annual weeds disappear with the mowing), couch or other perennial grasses present a continuing difficulty unless dealt with beforehand. The weeds will only be affected by glyphosate when they are growing vigorously, so begin in late spring and spend two or three months – applying the chemical every two weeks – ensuring that the task is done properly.

The site for the lawn need not be flat; a *gentle* slope is both acceptable and, in some respects, aesthetically desirable. It is extremely difficult to remove extensive humps and hollows once a lawn is established, so the site should be graded to

obtain a flat or *uniformly* sloping surface beforehand. After grading, the whole site must be levelled and firmed. The spring-tine lawn rake is the most effective tool for levelling and removing stones and clods of soil; rake in two alternate directions at right angles or you may introduce or accentuate, rather than diminish, humps and hollows. Firming is a tedious task, most efficiently performed by many pairs of feet shod in Wellington boots (rubbers); there are no shortcuts and a garden roller is not recommended as it can easily form humps and hollows too. About a week before you lay the lawn, scatter autumn lawn fertilizer over the area at the rate of approximately 68 g per sq m (2 oz per sq yd); although you are doing the job in spring, it is important to use a blend of fertilizer relatively low in nitrogen content.

Thus far, the preparation is the same whether you use turf or seed. The choice between the two is most likely to be made on grounds of cost. Seed is certainly cheaper but it is much more chancey and, of course, much slower to produce an end result. I would always opt for turf but advise you most strongly to avoid anything described as 'meadow turf'. This may be excellent for grazing cattle but is not the stuff of a garden lawn, and the designation 'weed-treated' is certainly no

indication that any weeds the meadow turf contains have actually been controlled. Instead, spend a little more on specially grown turf, which is widely available.

Many gardeners, of course, will prefer to use seed. For the best results, sow the seed on a day that is warm, moist and fairly windless. Most seed companies provide some form of measure or dosing device to indicate the amount of seed to apply per sq m (sq yd). The measure will be easiest to use if you divide up the prepared area with canes and string into metre (yard) squares. After sowing, rake very lightly over the area and then firm the soil with the back of a rake. Suspend lightweight plastic netting over the newly sown seeds to protect them from birds.

Turfs should be laid off-set from each other, like bricks in a wall. Stand on a plank laid on the prepared ground as you work, moving it as necessary. Place the new turfs in position and tamp down with the back of a rake. Do not lay small pieces of turf at the edges: always use a larger piece at the edge and insert infilling pieces towards the centre. Trim the edge with a half-moon edging knife.

After sowing or turfing, apply water by sprinkler at regular intervals to ensure that the soil does not dry out. If you have sown seed, use a very fine spray in order not to wash the seeds into dense groups.

A lawn should be much more than just a summer feature. If it is well-maintained it will be a year-round, constant asset in the changing landscape of the garden. As the daffodils herald the beginning of growth at the start of the season (*above left*), the lawn is just beginning to stir. Two or three months later the task of mowing is more than repaid by the deep green of a healthy sward (*above*), bordered by a mass of spring blossom.

Planting bulbs a little way back from the edge of the lawn (*left*) reduces the risk of damage to border plants during mowing and makes trimming the edges of the lawn much easier.

Climbing Plants for Spring

For me, spring is as much about early-flowering clematis and honeysuckle as it is bulbs and biennials. Making use of the vertical dimension not only increases gardening space but also enables you to savour the delights of some of the most beautiful and spectacular of ornamental plants. Most gardens have some unclothed verticals, be they house walls, boundary walls, fences or even trees and hedges. All can – and should – be embellished with climbing plants, and there is much to be said for erecting structures, such as archways, pergolas or pillars, specifically to support climbers within the garden itself.

In planning which climbers to choose, the most important consideration is the direction in which the vertical support faces – many of the best species require the warmth reflected from a south or south-west face in the Northern Hemisphere (north or north-east in the Southern Hemisphere). Even 'wrong'-facing walls are not the horticultural Eiger they might seem. It is the rapidity with which frozen tissues thaw out in the winter that limits the range of plants that will grow in cold sites, not the actual cold itself. A wall that is struck by the first rays only of the winter sun will generally present the greatest difficulty.

Growing plants against walls requires a little special care. The soil close to any vertical support will be drier than that in the open garden, so the site must be well prepared before planting. An area approx-imately 1 metre (3 ft) in diameter should be double dug and compost or manure, dusted with bone-meal, forked in thoroughly. After planting, you should water regularly throughout the drier times of the year and apply a thick surface mulch of organic matter at the beginning of the season to retain moisture. Because plants take up nutrients less efficiently from dry soil, I always give climbers a liquid feed regularly throughout the growing season.

Gardeners are often concerned about the possible damage that self-clinging plants, particularly ivy, can do to the brickwork of a house. In practice, damage is only likely to occur on old walls with crumbly bricks and loose lime mortar; modern bricks and mortar should not be

The original supporting structure has completely disappeared beneath a dramatic display of smoky-blue ceanothus (*far left*).

A rain-like cascade of laburnum (*left*) leads the eye downwards and towards the figure at the end of the path.

Wisteria, *Clematis montana*, ivy, camellia and *Cerastium tomentosum* (*left*) put on a spring show. Wisteria is often called the 'Queen of Climbers'. It is long lived and develops a stout branch system that requires the minimum of support against a house or other wall.

affected. In fact, a greater risk is presented by allowing vigorous species of clematis, wisterias and similar rampant species to force their shoots beneath roofing tiles or slates. If possible, never encourage any climbing plant (other than the few self-clinging species such as ivies or climbing hydrangea) to grow directly on the wall itself. Fix trellis supported on wooden battens approximately 5 cm (2 in) away from the wall; over a larger area, use a framework of wires strained from masonry nails or similar supports. In this way, the air can circulate freely around the plants, discouraging the pests and diseases that thrive in stagnant conditions.

But even with these precautions, climbers are more likely to have problems than most other plants because of the sheltered environment: climbing roses will almost invariably be more mildewed than bush roses. It is likely, therefore, that pest and disease control measures will need to be applied more frequently.

There is much to be said for choosing climbing plants that require the minimum of pruning: not only can it be difficult to prune without cutting the training wires (and ruining your secateurs) but often the operation must be done when perched precariously on a step-ladder. Most of the species that are grown for their foliage – such as ivies and parthenocissus vines – look after themselves, although occasionally they may need restraining. A few of the 'wilder' types of flowering climber

also require little pruning – either because, like the star jasmine *Trachelospermum*, they are slow growing, or because, like honeysuckles, they are best grown in a semi-natural woodland situation, given free rein to scramble over trees.

Among the remainder, two large and important groups of flowering climbers – roses and clematis – require rather careful pruning if they are to give of their best (see Spring Tasks **18**). Both fall into several groups. With the exception of ramblers, most roses are really climbing plants that are also grown as bushes or shrubs and their pruning reflects this. The pruning of the different types of clematis is dictated by the time of their flowering and the vigour of their growth.

The Alpine Garden

The appeal of alpine plants and of rock gardens was discovered relatively late in gardening history. Indeed, Reginald Farrer who is often referred to as the 'father of rock gardening' died as recently as 1920. And, in recent years, there has been a revolution in the ways in which alpine plants are grown: they do not have to be confined to a small-scale reproduction of a mountain range, even to a conventional rock garden. But to grow alpine plants successfully, it must be appreciated that, although belonging to a vast range of botanical families, ecologically they are rather a special group with a rather curious natural habitat.

Although called alpines, the plants that we now group under this name originate from a much wider range of localities than the European alps. Reginald Farrer was responsible for collecting vast numbers of Asiatic species and introducing them into cultivation. All the alpines share high-altitude homes with extremes of climatic conditions. Generally, soil is sparse or almost non-existent, rainfall is high but drains away very rapidly, and winds are strong and almost incessant. The temperature range is vast: not only does it vary from that prevailing during the perma-frost, or continuous deep snow cover of winter, to that associated with the bright clear sunlight of an often short summer, but the diurnal range is also enormous. Anyone who has tramped up quite a low mountain in the daytime and then camped on it overnight will know how the temperature plummets as the sun sets. Most often, it is after the snow has melted and the temperatures warm up in the spring that alpine plants are most beautiful.

The key to a successful alpine garden is a setting that looks reasonably natural (*above*). Changes in level are essential to create the cascading effect which shows alpine plants at their best, as they tumble over boulders and cling in nooks and crannies.

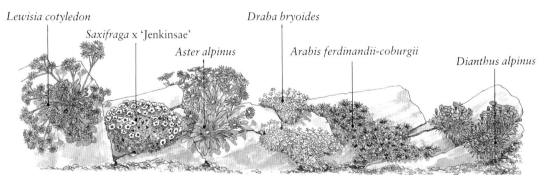

Lewisia cotyledon

Saxifraga x 'Jenkinsae'

Aster alpinus

Draba bryoides

Arabis ferdinandii-coburgii

Dianthus alpinus

In planning an alpine garden all the curious features of their environment must be borne in mind. Contrary to popular belief, alpines tolerate high temperatures but dislike clinging dampness, poorly drained soil or compost and inadequate ventilation. However, they are much less stunted and can often attain a luxuriance unseen in the wild state when grown in areas that are not subject to constant gales. The required conditions can be met in three main ways.

The first is in an alpine house: in essence, a cold greenhouse in which most, if not all, of the vents can be opened and which functions rather like a giant cloche. The staging must be robust enough to support a bed of free-draining gravel, on which to stand the plants in pots. The individual pots can be plunged up to their rims in the gravel for the best and most attractive results. Fill the pots with very gritty and free-draining compost; you can use specially formulated alpine compost, or a mixture comprising three parts (by volume) of John Innes No 2 soil-based potting compost, one part horticultural grit, one part peat and one part well-shredded leaf-mould.

The traditional method for growing alpines outdoors is in a rock garden. In practice, however, it is extremely difficult to build such a garden that looks pleasing. A successful rock garden must appear as if it occurred naturally. The type of rock should be local, and, if it occurs in obvious bedding planes or strata, these must all be laid in the same direction and be part buried, appearing as if dipping into the ground. Preferably, the garden should be built into the side of a slope

Helianthemum 'Wisley Primrose' grows easily in crevices (*left*).

Helichrysum milfordii (*below*) produces daisy-like white flowers.

rather than on flat ground (a heap of rocks can look ridiculous). When building a rock garden, excavate the area first to a depth of about 30 cm (12 in) and lay bricks or other rubble to ensure good drainage, remove all traces of perennial weeds from the site and then put the rocks in place, mixing liberal quantities of grit, peat and leaf-mould with the garden soil as you fill in around them. Allow several months for the rock garden to settle (filling in with more soil and grit mixture as necessary) before introducing plants.

The most practical and aesthetically pleasing way of growing alpine plants is in troughs or raised beds. Without attempting to provide a supposedly 'natural' environment or going to the expense of using an alpine house (which, in any case,

isolates the plants from the remainder of the garden) the plants are raised slightly from ground level and, therefore, are more readily visible. The retaining walls of the raised bed may be of stone, wood (logs or old railway sleepers) or peat blocks. The height above the surrounding soil should be at least 20 cm (8 in) and, as with a rock garden, the bed must first be excavated before refilling. The infilling soil can be mixed with lime chippings or be primarily a soil and peat mixture, depending on whether you are intending to grow lime-loving or lime-hating species. On a smaller scale, troughs can be of natural stone or one of the excellent modern substitutes; again, fill them with a medium to suit the types of plant that you choose to grow.

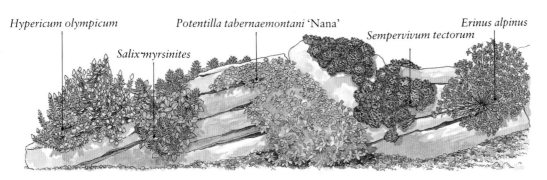

Hypericum olympicum

Salix myrsinites

Potentilla tabernaemontani 'Nana'

Sempervivum tectorum

Erinus alpinus

The choice of alpine plants is vast (*left*) and even within the major types the variety of growing conditions required is considerable. It makes sense, therefore, to buy from a nursery or garden centre which has a large range of clearly labelled plants.

The Water Garden

The gentle babble of a fountain, a small waterfall or even the contented plop of goldfish breaking the water's surface adds an extra dimension to any garden. And I do mean *any* garden – none is so small that space cannot be found for some aquatic feature. In spring the pond bursts into vibrant activity after its winter sulk (although the best way to maintain a pool free of ice is to keep a fountain running all year round). Plants are best planted and divided in late spring, but a new pond requires about a month in which to settle before life of any sort is introduced. The initial hole should be excavated early in the season when the soil is easy to work.

Concrete-lined ponds are not as popular nowadays as they once were. Not only are they troublesome to construct, but the concrete is prone to crack and it is difficult to seal the leaks. Of the modern materials, I advise strongly against polyethylene sheeting which has a limited life. Instead, opt for butyl rubber, a much more durable material that is very easy to lay. For very small ponds, pre-formed glass-fibre liners are a possibility, although these are generally pale in colour, and therefore difficult to disguise.

Whichever type of pond you choose, the criteria for the site are the same. Because water plants require about eight hours of direct sunlight each day, an open situation away from any shade is essential. Ideally, the position should also be well clear of deciduous trees: autumn leaves sink and decompose at the bottom of the pond, thereby depleting the water of oxygen and adding noxious and toxic gases. The site should also be level. If the garden slopes, the pond is better sited on the highest rather than the lowest ground, unless you plan a semi-natural pond and a surrounding bog garden: then you could allow the water to run down the slope to overflow from the pond into the area around. The choice between such a semi-natural pool and a more formal one should be made at an early stage – an informal pool surrounded by an Italianate courtyard could look rather inappropriate.

Having chosen the site, mark out on the

Even a relatively formal pond (*left*) is enhanced by the softening effects of planting around its edges. The site for a pond should in general, however, be as open as possible. Overhanging trees or shrubs block out the sunlight which water plants need in order to thrive, as well as causing problems through fallen leaves decomposing on the bottom.

ground the shape of the pond (use a hose-pipe for curves). To work out the size of rubber sheet needed, measure a rectangular area at least 50 cm (20 in) beyond its limits. Dig the pool hole to a depth of at least 45 cm (18 in) and preferably 50 cm (20 in): this depth is essential to enable fish to survive the winter. Leave a ledge (or a series of ledges if the pool is large enough) around the margin to allow for planting species that thrive in slightly shallower water. Finally, line the entire hole with about 5 cm (2 in) of sand to provide a smooth surface on which to bed the rubber liner – one jagged stone can cause a costly puncture.

Spread the rubber sheet over the hole, anchor it temporarily at the edges and then slowly fill the pond with water. As the water flows in, the rubber will stretch to fit the shaped hole: if necessary, adjust the anchoring weights slightly to prevent undue stress from developing. When the pond is full, permanently anchor the sheet at the edges – either with slabs for a formal pool, or with more irregular stones and soil for a semi-natural one. And then allow about a month for the whole to settle down before introducing plants and, after several more weeks, fish.

The easiest way to grow plants in the pond is in plastic planting baskets filled with garden soil. Choose soil that has not been heavily fertilized (and avoid vegetable plot soil) and do not use any organic manures or composts which, like

Numbers of plants for ponds of different sizes

Type of plant	Small pond (c 1.75 m × 1.25 m) 5½ ft × 4 ft	Medium pond (c 3 m × 1.75 m) 9¾ ft × 5½ ft	Large pond (c 3 m × 4.25 m) 9¾ ft × 14 ft
Oxygenating plants	10 bunches	25 bunches	80 bunches
Marginal plants	3	8	20
Floating plants	1	2	6
Water lilies	2 small varieties	2 small + 2 fairly vigorous varieties	4 small + 4 fairly vigorous varieties

Water can be used to create a wealth of imaginative effects in different environments. A simple, circular pond (*left*) adds interest in a large expanse of lawn and creates a focus for a sitting area.

A fountain (*below left*), framed by the lush foliage of hostas, brings a note of calm to a small town garden.

A semi-natural pond (*below*), with appropriately informal foliage and flowers tumbling over its edges, creates a secluded romantic haven.

autumn leaves, decompose and foul the water. Place a layer of gravel over the surface of the soil because fish – inquisitive things – tend to stir it up, sometimes dislodging the plants. As well as plants chosen for their beauty, you also need submerged oxygenating plants. In all plantings it is essential that the numbers and types of plant are appropriate to the dimensions of the pond (see left).

It is important, too, to introduce the right proportion of fish and a population of snails. Select goldfish, golden orfe or shubunkins rather than species such as carp and tench which constantly stir up mud and plants. In deciding on numbers, I work to 2.5 cm (1 in) of fish (excluding tail) per 4.5 litres (1 gallon) of water.

The New Season's Vegetables

The vegetables that we can pick or cut fresh from the garden in the spring share one of two attributes. Either they are long-term, fairly slow-growing crops that have been in the ground through the winter, or they are very fast-growing ones sown or planted out as soon as the soil has begun to warm up. Perhaps the most important of the long-term crops are two of the relatively few truly perennial vegetables, asparagus and rhubarb. If you plan the vegetable garden, as you should, on at least some sort of rotational basis (see page 17), these perennial types are among those that really must be left out of the rotational scheme altogether. Therefore, in deciding where to position them, choose a spot where their presence will not interfere with other vegetable garden operations. At one side or corner of the plot would be an ideal position.

There is little point in growing asparagus if you do not have permanent space to devote to it. In order to provide sufficient for two meals per week for a family of four over the short, six-week cutting season, you need about 48 plants. And if these are spaced according to the most modern practice, in a bed, 1 m (3 ft) wide with 30 cm (12 in) between plants, the total area needed will be around 7 sq m (8⅓ sq yd). The site should be in full sun and the soil thoroughly prepared: all perennial weeds such as couch or ground elder must be removed, the bed double dug and liberal quantities of well-rotted manure or compost incorporated. I recommend planting 'Connover's Colossal', which is an old but reliable variety; if at all possible, you should purchase two-year-old, container-raised crowns.

Rhubarb is a much simpler proposition than asparagus and one clump, occupying perhaps 0.25 sq m (⅓ sq yd), will be enough to satisfy even the most avowed addict. But it is a mistake to believe that rhubarb is wholly self-sufficient. To obtain a larger crop and more succulent sticks, dig in compost or manure before planting and then provide similar organic matter as a mulch.

Although by the end of the summer, many gardeners have begun to tire of lettuce, the first outdoor plants in the spring are a different matter altogether and their maturity is awaited eagerly. Lettuce is a versatile plant and grows well in most soils, although it is prone to suffer from slug damage on wet sites. The sweetest, tenderest leaves and hearts always come from plants grown in a sunny position on a fairly free-draining soil and given generous watering. The easiest way

to grow lettuce is in a bed devoted to the various types – butterhead, crisp, cos (romaine), cut-and-come-again and red varieties – but, if space is limited, the alternative is to intercrop. This means sowing or planting a row of lettuces in between other, larger but slower-growing plants such as Brussels sprouts before they cast too much shade: the small butterhead variety 'Tom Thumb' and the cos 'Little Gem' are ideal in limited spaces. Determine how many heads you will need every ten days or so and sow slightly more than this number (to allow for losses) each time the seedlings from the previous sowing have emerged above soil level.

Being very fast growing, spinach also makes an excellent plant for intercropping. It is fairly unusual among vegetables in having moderate tolerance of shade, which is another good reason for using it to occupy the ground between rows of taller plants. Allow sufficient space to sow a row about 4 m (13 ft) long every three weeks. If you have a very small garden, you could grow one of the plants that can be used instead of true spinach, Swiss chard. Its leaf blade makes a very acceptable substitute (and the thick white vein an alternative to sea kale) but only four or six plants would be needed as the leaves are large and rapidly replaced. Choose a sunny site and well-manured soil; being larger plants than real spinach, they are not as suitable for intercropping.

Some gardeners obtain supplies of spring onions (scallions) from the thinnings of a bulb onion crop, but it is much better and more reliable to sow a variety such as 'White Lisbon' especially for the purpose. As with all onions, a well-manured site is important. The commonest failures arise when the seed has been sown into poor soil and/or the plants have been allowed to dry out. Spring onions have the additional advantage of taking up very little garden room: permit sufficient space to sow a single row about 2 m (6½ ft) long every month. Allow about 10 cm (4 in) either side of the row, which you will have to hand-weed; onions are shallow-rooted and are liable to be damaged if you use a hoe near them.

Spinach is ideal for intercropping as it is moderately tolerant of shade and can therefore be grown next to tall-growing plants such as runner beans (*above*).

A large garden allows the luxury of a well-spaced vegetable plot (*left*) but for those with less room to spare, careful planning and organization of rows are essential.

Growing your own vegetables should not mean a glut of monotonous produce. Sow different varieties of lettuce (*top*) so that you can ring the changes throughout the season.

Swiss chard (*above*) is an ideal vegetable for a small garden. Its spinach-like leaves are large and they will replace themselves rapidly after each picking.

SPRING TASKS

1. Mark out the boundary with string and pegs and lay the turfs close together. In alternate rows begin with a half turf so the edges are staggered and therefore more stable.

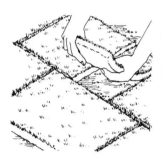

2. A small piece of turf at the end of a row may break away, so lay a whole piece at the edge and fill in elsewhere in the row with a smaller piece.

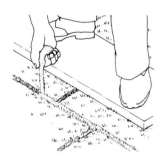

3. Fill in the gaps between the turfs with fine soil to create a level surface. The pressure of your feet could damage the new turf so always stand on a plank or board to even out your weight.

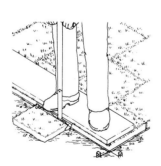

4. Wait until the turf has settled then, again standing on a board, trim the edges of the outside turfs by making a cut sloping slightly away from you. Wait 10 to 14 days before mowing the new lawn.

1 Lawns: maintenance

At the start of the season, lawns should be lightly raked or brushed to disperse worm casts and collect up twigs and other winter debris. As long as the weather is not frosty lawns may be cut, but with the mower blades set as high as possible.

In the second half of the season, apply spring lawn fertilizer. Wait until the weather is fairly warm as most spring lawn fertilizers include a weedkiller which is ineffective in cold weather.

2 Lawns: sowing or turfing

Mid season is an excellent time to sow or turf a new lawn. Prepare the soil as for an ornamental bed (see **32**), although the best pre-sowing or turfing fertilizer is one of the proprietary blends sold as autumn/winter lawn feed. Make sure there are no humps or hollows and sow the seed uniformly (most seed suppliers include some sprinkling device to ensure both uniformity and correct density of seed). Cover the seeds lightly with peat or fine soil and firm the area by treading. Fruit cage netting supported over the seed bed will deter birds.

Lay turf as shown.

3 Weeds: hoeing

On warm dry days, use a Dutch or similar hoe to control weeds among ornamentals and vegetables. Do not hoe close to soft fruit bushes and canes, or onions, all of which are particularly prone to surface root damage.

4 Weeds: applying weedkillers

Weedkillers may be applied as necessary to the garden in the second half of the season as the weather and soil warm up. Always check carefully that the weedkiller is appropriate for the task: it is easy to damage plants by using a total, or persistent product where a selective, or non-persistent, one is required.

5 Ponds: planting

Towards the end of the season, plant or divide water lilies and other pond plants. Choose varieties that are appropriate to the size and depth of the pond; plant them in baskets, and use garden soil to which no organic matter or fertilizers have been added recently (a sachet of water plant food may be placed in the base of each basket, however).

5 A ledge in your pond will enable you to plant species which like differing depths of water. Using bricks as a base is an alternative method. Proprietary plastic planting baskets are ideal containers, as they let in light and air and have the added advantage of keeping the roots of rapidly-spreading plants such as water lilies under control.

Greenhouse

6 | Shading

Apply specially formulated, white shade paint (available at garden supply centres) to the outside of the glass as soon as the inside temperatures begin to exceed about 20°C (70°F) during the daytime; clean the glass before applying the paint. At about the same time, remove bubble film plastic insulation and store it safely until autumn.

7 | Ventilation

As the greenhouse warms up, open the ventilators in the daytime, partly for cooling but also to prevent a buildup of moisture and to admit fresh air for plant growth. Automatic vents are a wise investment if you are often away from home.

8 | House plants: sowing

Take the opportunity, before plant-raising space is occupied with the bulk of the hardy plants, to raise some house plants from seed. *Coleus*, African violets and *Exacum* are among the most satisfactory and easy; surplus plants are always useful as gifts.

9 | Vegetable and ornamental plants: sowing

Sow seeds of hardy vegetable and ornamental plants as directed on seed packets: slower-growing types should, of course, be sown first. Almost all types give better results if they are raised indoors in this way and planted out later rather than being sown directly; however, root vegetables are exceptions for they don't transplant satisfactorily. But as space is likely to be limited, choose first those listed – these benefit most from a protected start. Ensure that seed trays and propagators have been washed out thoroughly, disinfected and then rinsed and always use fresh sowing compost.

10 | Pricking on

As seeds germinate and the seedlings emerge, they must be pricked on. Once two true leaves have expanded, most are robust enough to handle, although it is better if very fragile types such as lobelias are left a little longer and then pricked on in small clumps. Large plants are best pricked on into individual 7.5 cm (3 in) diameter pots, but smaller types, including most bedding plants, are more usefully transferred into further seed trays. Spacings of plants after pricking on will vary depending on the type of plant but about 3 cm (1 in) between each suits most.

11 | Hardening off

Three or four weeks before the last frosts are expected, move the young plants into the cold frame for hardening off.

12 | Vegetables: planting

When tomato, cucumber, pepper (capsicums) and aubergine (eggplant) plants are approximately 10 to 12 cm (4 to 5 in) tall, knock them from their pots and plant them into greenhouse beds, growing bags or, best of all, into ring culture pots. If you are planting into bags or pots of compost, bring these into the greenhouse about two weeks in advance of planting to allow the compost to warm up to the greenhouse temperature.

As the plants elongate, tie them in to canes or similar supports; tomatoes require re-tying almost weekly as growth speeds up towards early summer. Remove side-shoots from tomatoes and cucumbers; on tomatoes, this may need to become almost a daily operation. Feed them weekly with a proprietary liquid fertilizer and as the flowers form, tap the plants regularly around midday to help pollination. Remove any male flowers on older varieties of cucumber.

10 1. Seedlings can be pricked on once true leaves have developed. Make planting holes about 3 cm (1 in) apart.

2. Use a widger to remove the seedlings very carefully from their compost. Hold them by the leaf rather than by the stem.

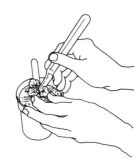

3. Larger plants should be transferred to individual 7.5 cm (3 in) diameter pots. Once the seedling is in place, firm down the soil around it with your fingers.

13 Grapevines

As soon as the greenhouse begins to warm up grapevines must be kept in check. If more than one side-shoot arises from each bud cluster on the main stem or rod, pinch out the weaker ones to leave two. Then pinch out the weaker of these when the side-shoots are about 10 cm (4 in). Tie the shoots in to wires on the roof as they grow; pinch out their tips once they reach their allotted length. Pinch out the sub-sideshoots that arise from them, pinching just above one leaf from their base.

14 Pests

Keep an eye open for the first signs of pest attack: a leaf bearing a few aphids can just be picked off, but regular spraying with a contact insecticide such as derris is required for dealing with white fly.

15 Fuchsias: cuttings

As potted, non-hardy fuchsias begin to stir into life after a winter under cover, cuttings may be taken from the shoot tips (which are, in any event, usefully removed to encourage bushiness). Dip the cuttings in rooting powder and place them in 7.5 cm (3 in) diameter pots under a bench-top propagator.

16 Peaches and nectarines: pollination

Peach and nectarine trees growing in greenhouses or conservatories require help with pollination. Make sure that the soil around the roots is not allowed to dry: mulching helps.

17 Ornamentals: re-potting

Perennial house and greenhouse ornamentals such as succulents, cacti and azaleas should be re-potted no more often than every three years. But when they become very pot bound, move them to a pot one size larger in mid spring. Pull away a little of the compost around the periphery of the root-ball, tease out the roots slightly and pack in fresh compost.

16

To increase the prospects of a good crop, help along the pollination of peaches and nectarines. Agitate the flowers very gently with a soft paint brush, ideally once a day (around noon is ideal) while the trees are flowering.

13 1. Once buds are beginning to swell on the main stem of the grapevine, remove all except two of the buds from each bud cluster.

2. As the young side-shoots begin to elongate from the two remaining buds, remove the weaker to leave one.

A greenhouse (*left*) can be much more than a purely functional structure. A peach tree in the greenhouse lights up the whole garden with its blossom in spring, at a time when many other plants and trees are still bare.

Trees and Shrubs

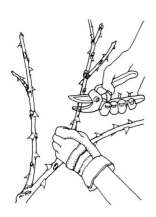

18 When pruning any variety of rose always make the cut just above an outward-facing bud.

18 Roses: pruning

As soon as the worst frosts are over, rose pruning can be undertaken. In all instances, make cuts to an outward-facing bud. On all plants, cut out very old, moribund shoots and any showing signs of disease lesions. On large-flowered bush roses (hybrid teas), cut all shoots back by about half (slightly more for weaker growing plants, slightly less for stronger growing plants). On cluster-flowered bush roses (floribundas), cut one third of all shoots back to the base and the remainder back by about one third (again, cutting more for weaker and less for stronger growing varieties): in this way, the entire plant will be rejuvenated on a three-year cycle. On shrub roses, cut out the very old shoots only and shorten any others damaged by winter winds. Miniature roses need merely a trimming back of frost-damaged shoots and a thinning out to ensure that the centre of the plant is not too congested. Climbing roses too can be pruned now and also any ramblers which were not pruned last autumn.

19 Shrubs: pruning

As mid season approaches, prune the slightly less hardy shrubs, such as outdoor fuchsias and hydrangeas, left unpruned in the autumn; cut out any dead or damaged shoots. Also cut back the dead flower heads on mop-head hydrangeas with three or four leaves attached or, if there are plenty of strong, non-flowering shoots, cut them right back to the base.

Many shrubs that flower in the spring should be pruned as the flowers fade. The amount of pruning necessary varies.

20 Shrubs: feeding

As roses and other flowering shrubs start growing, give each a top-dressing of a proprietary rose fertilizer, following the manufacturer's instructions. After feeding, top up any organic mulch applied in the autumn or mulch afresh as necessary.

21 Heathers: cutting back

Towards the end of the season, as the bloom fades on winter-flowering heathers, cut back the dead flowering shoots hard to stimulate fresh growth. The easiest way to do this is with single-handed shears.

22 Trees: planting

Planting of bare-rooted trees should be completed by early spring, but mid season is an excellent time to plant those from containers. Prepare a planting hole approximately twice the volume of the container and fork in well-rotted manure or compost and a scattering of bone-meal. Tease out the roots slightly from the edges of the root-ball before planting and firm them in carefully afterwards. For young trees install a stake and a belt-pattern tie.

23 Roses: spraying

Towards the end of the season, spray roses with a proprietary mixture of insecticide and fungicide to control aphids, mildew and black spot.

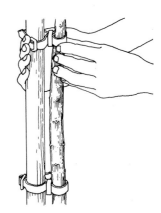

22 With young trees it is very important to provide proper support from the outset. The best method is to install a stake with belt-pattern ties at the top and bottom.

---

19 **Common spring-flowering shrubs to be pruned after the flowers fade:**

Berberis Thin old wood, cut back old plants fairly hard.
Calluna Clip back hard all flowering shoots.
Camellia Lightly shape only.
Chaenomeles Cut out very old wood, shorten long shoots.
Choisya Cut back oldest third of shoots to ground level.
Clematis Prune lightly: remove weak or overgrown shoots.
Cytisus Trim lightly, do not cut into old wood.
Erica Trim hard with shears.
Forsythia Cut out oldest wood every 3-4 years; prune wall-trained shrubs to a young shoot from previous year.
Jasmine Cut back flowering shoots to two buds above base. Large wall-trained plants can be clipped hard.

Other Ornamentals

24 | Snowdrops and aconites: moving

Move and divide snowdrops and aconites while they are still in full leaf at the start of the season: they can be hard to re-establish or reluctant to flower if moved after the foliage has died down.

25 | Lilies: feeding

At the start of the season, apply a top-dressing and mulch to lilies, those in pots and in the open garden; use well-rotted leaf-mould to which bone-meal has been added at the rate of about one handful per gallon (4.5 litres) of mulch.

26 | Herbaceous perennials: moving

Divide and move large clumps of herbaceous perennials, especially less hardy types such as peonies, just as they start to grow at the start of the season: if they are moved any later, when well into growth, flowering may be lost for this year.

27 | Herbaceous perennials: feeding

Apply a top-dressing of blood, fish and bone fertilizer around established herbaceous perennials as soon as they begin to grow. Apply slug pellets around delphiniums, primulas and other types that experience has shown to be particularly prone to attack in your garden.

28 | Herbaceous perrenials: staking

Stake tall-growing herbaceous perennials, such as lupins and delphiniums, as soon as the flower stems begin to elongate: a bend, once acquired, is impossible to correct. And clumps of bushy perennials such as hardy geraniums should be restricted to prevent them from flopping. Modern interlocking supports of plastic-coated wire are excellent for both purposes.

29 | Bearded irises: spraying

Once the new leaves on bearded irises are about 15 cm (6 in) tall, spray with a copper-containing fungicide to protect against leaf spot problems.

30 | Sweet peas: planting out

Early in the season, plant out sweet peas that were sown last autumn and overwintered in the cold frame. If no trench has been prepared, dig well-rotted manure or compost in to the planting area and apply a dressing of bone-meal at about 68 g per sq m (2 oz per sq yd) as you do so. Place one plant on each side of bamboo canes arranged in a row with 15 cm (6 in) between each cane; alternatively, plant them in pairs, about 15 cm (6 in) apart around a 2 m (2 yd) high wigwam of twigs. From mid season onwards, sweet peas may be sown directly in the garden, but the results will almost always be less satisfactory.

31 | Rock garden plants: checking

Make routine checks of alpine and other rock garden plants. Pull away dead leaves, re-firm any plants loosened by rain or frost, apply slug pellets around rock primulas and other species with soft foliage, and scatter coarse grit around plants bearing flower buds to lessen the chances of rotting or other damage to the blooms.

32 | Soil: preparing beds

Towards mid season, prepare the soil in beds and borders where annuals are to be planted or sown. Use a fork to break down large clods still remaining after the winter and remove any weeds. About two weeks before the sowings or plantings, gently rake the beds to prepare a fine tilth (doing this any earlier is pointless for heavy rain can easily pound the fine surface and render it impervious); as annuals are often

28 | Tall herbaceous perennials need proper support if they are to grow straight and not acquire an unattractive bend. It is easy to provide this with plastic-coated, linked wire supports.

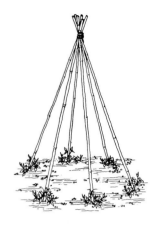

30 | One method of supporting sweet peas is to plant them in pairs, about 15 cm (6 in) apart, around a 2 m (2 yd) high wigwam of canes or twigs. This may be easier to accommodate in an area where space is limited than the alternative method based on rows of canes.

placed between perennials, a small garden rake is generally the easiest tool to use for this. At the same time as you rake, scatter blood, fish and bone fertilizer over the soil at the rate of 68 g per sq m (2 oz per sq yd).

33 | Soil: warming

After initial preparation, the soil should be warmed before the seeds are sown, to encourage swifter and more uniform germination: the simplest way to do this is by placing individual cloches over the soil. Once the seeds are sown the cloches can be replaced to protect the young seedlings. As seedlings emerge, thin them out to the spacings recommended on the packets.

34 | Annuals: hardening off

Around mid season, as hardy and half-hardy annuals reach a height of 4 to 5 cm (1½ to 2 in), move them into a cold frame for hardening off: allow a minimum of two weeks (and remember that, even then, half-hardy plants cannot be planted out until the danger of frost has passed). In the first week, leave the frame half-open in the daytime but fully closed at night; in the second week, leave it fully open in the daytime and half open at night.

35 | Annuals: planting out

From mid season onwards, plant out hardened-off hardy annuals raised in the greenhouse. Sow seed of hardy annuals, such as candytuft and alyssum, directly in their final growing positions.

36 | Corms and bulbs: planting out

From mid season onwards, plant gladiolus corms at weekly intervals to ensure a succession of flowers. Dig down 9 to 11 cm (3½ to 4½ in), allowing a similar distance between holes. Add

about 1 cm (½ in) of horticultural sand to which bone-meal has been added at the rate of approximately a handful per gallon (4.5 litres) of sand; this will lessen the chances of rotting. Lay the corms on the sand and cover with soil. Hardy summer- and autumn-flowering corms and bulbs can be planted similarly, adjusting the planting depth and spacing as suppliers recommend; particularly useful types include 'De Caen' and 'St Brigid' anemones, alliums, cyclamen, some irises, nerines and tricyrtis.

37 | Dahlias: planting out

About five weeks before the last frost is expected, remove dahlia tubers from storage and plant them out. Make sure that the tops of the crowns are approximately 10 cm (4 in) below the soil surface, and scatter bone-meal around them as you plant. Insert a stake *before* filling the planting hole to avoid damage.

38 | Chrysanthemums: planting out

About three weeks before the last frost is expected, plant out outdoor chrysanthemums.

39 | Containers: preparing for bedding plants

Towards the end of the season, prepare containers for summer bedding plants, first removing bulbs for drying and also the remains of any early hardy ornamentals such as wallflowers. Re-fill small containers with fresh potting compost and replace the top 5 to 8 cm (2 to 3 in) of compost in larger tubs.

40 | Bulbs: cutting back

Cut off the dead flower heads of daffodils, narcissi and other early-flowering bulbs as they fade. Then apply liquid fertilizer but do not cut back the foliage until six weeks after the end of flowering.

32 Once the soil is dry enough, prepare beds and borders for planting.

1. Loosen the soil with a fork, breaking down clods and removing weeds.

2. Two weeks before sowing or planting, rake the soil to prepare a fine tilth.

37 Dig a hole approximately 15 cm (6 in) deep and insert a stake. Scattering bone-meal in the hole, put in the dahlia tubers with the crown (the base of the old stem) against the stake and approximately 10 cm (4 in) below the surface of the soil. A distance of 0.75 to 1 m (2 to 3 ft) between plants and between rows will suit most dahlias.

Fruit

41 Planting

Complete the planting of bare-rooted trees, bushes and canes by very early spring when growth begins again. Plants raised in containers can be transplanted at any time if they are well watered in. Apply an organic mulch if this has not been done already.

42 Feeding

At the very start of the season, apply a top-dressing of sulphate of potash at the rate of about 17 g per sq m (½ oz per sq yd) around cane and bush fruit and young trees. Follow this with a layer of organic mulch, either compost or well-rotted manure. Then, in mid season, apply blood, fish and bone fertilizer at the same rate of 17 g per sq m (½ oz per sq yd).

43 Young trees: protecting

On young apple and pear trees growing near to older, scab-affected trees, apply a protective spray with benomyl, thiophanate-methyl or carbendazim fungicide as the buds burst. Repeat this as the young leaves unfold, again when the flower buds are swelling, and finally after the petals drop. The later sprays also give some protection against mildew.

44 Figs: pruning

Prune wall-trained figs in mid season once the danger of very hard frosts has passed. Cut out any shoots growing directly towards or away from the wall and any that have been killed or damaged by winter cold. Thin out the remainder by cutting out each alternate shoot, keeping as many as possible of those that bear most embryo figs at their tips. In all cases, cut back to just above one bud from the shoot base.

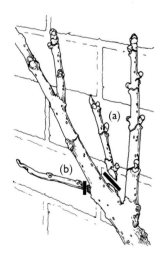

44 Figs produce fruit on the current year's growth so some older branches must be cut back. Before thinning out remove any shoots growing directly towards or away from the wall (a) and any damaged over winter (b).

45 Peaches and almonds: leaf curl disease

As the leaves unfold on peach and almond trees, apply a second protective spray with a copper-containing fungicide to guard against leaf curl disease (see AUTUMN TASKS **52**).

46 Peaches and nectarines: pruning

Prune wall-trained peaches and nectarines just after growth begins. Later, at the end of spring, when the fruits have set and reached the size of walnuts, thin out the fruits to leave one every 10 cm (4 in).

47 Peaches and nectarines: pollinating

Peach or nectarine trees growing against walls require help with pollination: agitate the flowers with a very soft paintbrush (see **16**). Make sure that the soil around the roots is not allowed to dry out: mulching helps.

46 Just after growth begins on wall-trained peaches and nectarines, cut back to two leaves those shoots which have flower buds at the base. Shoots growing directly towards or away from the wall should also be removed.

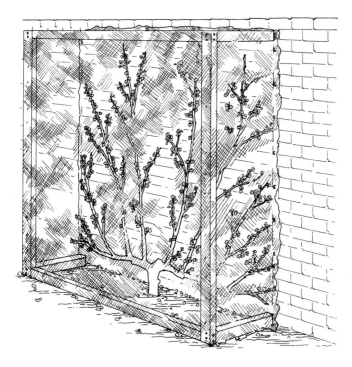

51 Canes: cutting back

Cut back the frost-damaged tips of raspberry canes to about 15 cm (6 in) above the top training wire (which should be 1.8 to 2 m [6 to 6½ ft] high). Thin the numbers of new canes to leave six to eight per plant by *pulling* out the weaker ones and those furthest from the row; re-tie the canes as necessary.

Thin the numbers of canes on blackberries, loganberries and other hybrid berries to leave five to six per plant; re-tie the canes as necessary in a fan pattern.

52 Raspberries: spraying

Spray raspberry canes with fenitrothion about one month before the last frosts are expected; repeat this two weeks later to control cane midge, a pest which predisposes plants to attack from cane blight and spur blight diseases.

53 Strawberries: protecting

Place cloches over strawberry plants early in the season to advance the maturity of the crop and protect the blossom from frost damage.

Feed the plants with a mixture of equal parts of bonemeal and sulphate of potash at about 17 g per sq m (½ oz per sq yd). Towards the end of the season, as strawberry fruits begin to set, cover with netting any plants not protected by cloches.

54 Plums: pruning

Towards the end of the season, prune established wall-trained plums (free-standing trees need little attention). Cut out all shoots growing directly towards or away from the wall, as well as some of the side-shoots, to leave one every 10 cm (4 in). Stop the remaining side-shoots at a point just above six leaves from the base of the side-shoot.

49 Early blossom needs adequate protection

against frost. Lightweight netting or plastic sheet attached to a wooden frame or fastened in a roll to the wall above the plant can provide this. It is easy to move the frame into place or roll down the netting when frost is forecast.

48 Apples and pears: mildew

Carefully pinch off the first signs of mildew-affected leaves on apples and pears, without showering the white spores on to healthy foliage.

49 Wall-trained fruit: protecting blossom

Protect the blossom on early-flowering wall-trained fruit, such as peaches, nectarines and plums, by erecting lightweight close-woven netting or plastic sheet in front of them. Secure the netting or sheet to a light, wooden frame and place it in position whenever frosts are expected; alternatively, secure a roll of netting to the wall above the plants and roll it down.

50 Fruit cages: checking

Check the netting on fruit cages as the crops begin to set to ensure that it is bird-proof, particularly at ground level where birds can hop underneath.

53 1. Cloches will protect strawberry plants from frost and speed their growth.

2. Even if you do not use cloches early in the season, netting is essential once the fruits begin to set as protection against birds.

Vegetables

55 Soil: preparing

At the start of the season, prepare the soil for seed sowing. Remove weeds and use a fork to break down large clods still remaining after the winter. About two weeks before the first sowings are to be made, gently rake the plot to prepare a fine tilth (doing this any earlier is pointless for heavy rain can easily pound the fine surface and render it impervious). At the same time as you rake, scatter blood, fish and bone fertilizer over the soil at the rate of 70 g per sq m (2 oz per sq yd); immediately before sowing, you will need to apply more fertilizer but the amount varies, depending on the type of vegetable. Prepare the potato bed similarly.

56 Soil: warming

After initial preparation, the soil should be warmed before seeds are sown to encourage swifter and more uniform germination. Either place cloches over the soil where the seed drills will lie, or cover larger areas of the plot with plastic sheet, anchored at the edges. Once the seeds are sown, cloches can be replaced to protect the young seedlings; normal plastic sheet cannot be used in this way, but a lightweight, perforated plastic sheet is now available and many crops, such as potatoes and carrots, can grow beneath this, pushing it upwards as they do so.

57 Asparagus: planting out

Early in the season, prepare the asparagus bed, taking especial care to remove all perennial weeds. Plant out bought one-year-old crowns about one month later.

58 Root vegetables: sowing

Early in the season make the first sowings of root vegetables, especially beetroot, radishes and carrots. Choose fast-growing early varieties (bolt-resistant types in the case of beetroot) and sow sparingly to cut down the amount of thinning needed. This is essential for beetroot because each 'seed' is, in fact, a cluster of seeds and several seedlings come up at each position (thin out all but the strongest). It is important with carrots, too, because thinning out the plants disturbs the foliage, releasing an aroma which attracts the carrot fly pest. Continue to make further sowings at two- to three-week intervals.

59 Broad beans: planting out

From early in the season, plant out broad beans raised in the greenhouse and hardened off in the cold frame, and make the first outdoor sowings. Sow the seeds in blocks (rather than rows) with 25 cm (10 in) between sowing positions – sow the seeds in pairs approximately 5 cm (2 in) deep and, if both germinate, pull out the weaker seedling. Make further sowings at three-week intervals.

60 Lettuce: planting out and sowing

From early in the season, plant out summer lettuce raised in the greenhouse and hardened off in the cold frame, and make the first outdoor sowings. Sow the seeds about 2 cm (1 in) deep and in blocks with equal spacing between plants. The spacing should be about 25 cm (10 in) for small varieties and up to 35 cm (14 in) for large ones. Continue to sow a few more as the seedlings emerge.

61 Spring onions: sowing

Make the first sowings of spring onions from early in the season. Sow in rows approximately 10 cm (4 in) apart and try to space the plants approximately 1 cm (½ in) apart. Continue to make further sowings at two-week intervals.

57 It is important that the soil in which asparagus is planted is free from perennial weeds. Prepare a trench about 20 cm (8 in) deep, with a ridge in the bottom about 7.5 cm (3 in) high, and plant the asparagus crowns on this, with their roots spread out.

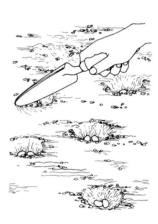

59 When planting broad beans sow the seeds in a chequerboard pattern. Dig holes at 25 cm (10 in) intervals, plant the seeds in pairs and cover with soil.

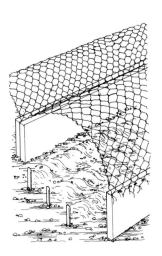

| 62 | 1. Support fine mesh chicken wire over rows of peas to provide protection from birds.

2. Remove the netting and insert twigs as support as soon as the seedlings emerge.

| 62 | Peas: sowing

Make the first sowings of peas from early in the season. Choose an early variety and sow approximately 4 cm (1½ in) deep and 12 cm (5 in) apart in three-banded rows, with 45 cm (18 in) between each triple row. Protect the seedlings from birds.

| 63 | Calabrese: sowing

Early in the season, sow calabrese in a small seed bed. When the plants are about 15 cm (6 in) tall, transplant them to their growing positions, allowing approximately 30 cm (12 in) between plants.

| 64 | Parsley: sowing

Early in the season, sow parsley in rows or small patches. Sow thinly and be prepared for slow and erratic germination.

| 65 | Kohlrabi and Swiss chard: sowing

In mid season, sow kohlrabi and Swiss chard. Both should be sown at a spacing of approximately 25 cm (10 in). Kohlrabi must be pulled when only a little larger than a golf ball for tenderness. Swiss chard is a plant from which leaves can be pulled repeatedly: as few as four or six plants are enough to supply the average family for the year.

| 66 | Herbs: planting out and sowing

In mid season, prepare and plant the herb bed with bought potted plants of lemon balm, bergamot, catmint, curry plant, rosemary, sages, thymes and other fairly woody perennials. Sow seed of annual herbs, such as basil, chervil, savory, in pots in the greenhouse or, towards the end of the season, outdoors under cloches. Sow seeds outdoors or plant bought pot plants of herbaceous perennial herbs such as chives, fennel, feverfew and mints.

| 67 | Potatoes: planting out

Plant the tubers of early potatoes in mid season with a spacing between plants of approximately 30 cm (12 in). As shoots emerge, cover them with soil to protect them from frost and then cover them again when about 25 cm (10 in) high; earthing up, as this is called, is important to prevent the tubers turning green and poisonous.

| 68 | Later sowings

About two to three weeks before the danger of frost passes, sow cucumbers, French beans, marrows, runner beans and sweet corn. Sow cucumbers or marrows in pairs 2.5 cm (1 in) deep, leaving 45 cm (18 in) between sowing positions; pull out the weaker seedling of each pair. Sow French beans 5 cm deep, with 15 cm (6 in) between plants. Sow runner beans in pairs at the bases of support canes, as described for sweet peas (see **30**). Always sow sweet corn in pairs 3 cm (1¼ in) deep and in blocks, with 35 cm (14 in) between each planting position; pull out the weaker seedling of each pair if both germinate.

| 69 | Greenhouse-raised seedlings

At the end of the season, cucumber, marrow, runner bean, sweet corn and tomato plants raised in the greenhouse can be planted out under the protection of cloches, using the same spacings as for outdoor sowings (see **68**). Tomatoes, which are only sown directly outdoors in very mild areas, should be planted in blocks 35 cm (14 in) apart if in the open ground, or in growing bags.

| 70 | Rhubarb and herbs: planting out and dividing

Plant rhubarb and divide clumps of non-woody perennial herbs, such as marjoram and mint.

| 67 | In mid season plant small (hen's egg sized) potato tubers at a depth of approximately 10 cm (4 in), with the sprouts, which should be about 0.5 to 1 cm (¼ to ½ in) long, uppermost.

SUMMER

The culmination of the gardener's year comes with the summer months. All the preparation of the previous seasons is rewarded with a wealth of fruit and vegetables ready to be gathered, roses in every colour, flourishing trees and shrubs, and beds and borders overflowing with flowers like this collection of helianthus, coreopsis, helenium and loosestrife in the colours of the sun.

SUMMER NOTES

The short space of time, just a few months, between the first days of spring and the height of summer sees plant growth on a scale that would be amazing were we not so accustomed to it – these Canterbury bells have grown from almost nothing to tall flower spikes, and the apple tree has covered itself in leaf and a fine crop of fruit.

How Plants Grow

Growth and growing are words used by gardeners almost daily. And as the summer progresses, the many manifestations of plant growth are apparent all around. Lawns require cutting twice a week if they are to look their best. Tomatoes and other vigorous vegetable crops are putting on new leaves, as are flowers and fruits at a prodigious pace. Even old-established perennials such as apple and pear trees produce an enormous weight of fresh foliage, flowers and fruit each season, not to mention a great additional weight and length of twigs and shoots. Yet how rarely do we question exactly what growth and growing mean?

I hope I shall not be accused of stating the obvious when I say that plants are unlike animals. For while, at the most fundamental levels of cellular activity, they have much in common, they feed in different ways and they grow very differently: whereas the whole body of an animal grows more or less uniformly, plants can grow only in certain specialized regions. These regions are called meristems. With grasses (see page 18), the meristem responsible for the elongation of grass stems is at the bottom, not the top of the plant. This is an exception, for almost all plants have these cells sited at the tip; the region is often referred to as an apical meristem. There are other meristems too, such as those responsible for radial growth that bring about thickening of stems (this type of meristem on tree trunks, for example, is the soft,

delicate layer of tissue immediately beneath the bark). During the summer, most meristems are working overtime, and the plants' needs for water and nutrients must be attended to.

But there is another difference between plant and animal growth, one that is rather more obvious. All parents know that animals (in the shape of their children) grow continuously in height and girth until their late teens, when this prodigious and very expensive process gradually slows down. Most human beings attain their full height around this time and, in a comparable way, dogs, horses and elephants – no matter how long they live – do not become larger and larger *ad infinitum*. Plants are different. They continue to grow throughout their lives and in a good summer they elongate and/or spread without pause. Ultimately, the growth of plants (within their basic annual, biennial or perennial life habit) is limited not so much by an inherited feature of their species but by diseases, pests or climate. In other words, a plant only stops growing – either upwards or sideways – when it begins to die.

Pollination

There is a vibrancy and there is certainly a humming in a summer garden anywhere that plants are blooming. Of course, the humming comes mainly from bees stimulated into activity by the heat, but there are many other types of insect abroad too: flies of many types, wasps, ants, cicadas, beetles and – most conspicuous yet silent – butterflies. At night-time, their places are taken mainly by moths but they are not alone in their actions.

We may think that butterflies enter the garden merely for our visual delight while other insects, wasps especially, do so simply to plague us. But there is a basic biological purpose to it all. The primary reason why insects visit gardens, and flowers in particular, is to seek food. Flowers produce nectar, a sugary, energy-rich secretion that is fondly sought by insects of many kinds. And as they dive into flowers to collect the nectar, insects transfer pollen from stamens to stigma, helping along the

Buddleia davidii, the butterfly bush, attracts insects and butterflies of many kinds to a garden, so aiding the pollination of other plant species.

49

process of pollination, which is the prelude to fertilization and ultimately seed production. Of course, it is a relatively simple task if the stamens and stigma are within the same flower, but often pollen must be transferred from one flower to another, either on the same plant or on a different one altogether. This cross-pollination may be necessary because individual flowers are unisexual or because, although bisexual, they are unable to be fertilized with their own pollen. Such factors are important in the pollination of fruit trees where two different trees are generally needed – often two of different yet compatible varieties.

Although insects are the most familiar carriers of pollen, other creatures can also effect pollination and, in tropical plants especially, birds, bats and slugs are among those playing important roles. Indeed, the sole reason plants have flowers of bright colours or alluring perfume is to attract small creatures that creep or fly – rather than humans.

In many gardens the wind is the second most important pollinating agent. Of course, the wind is not attracted to flowers in the way that insects or other animals are and the mechanism is somewhat different. Wind-pollinated plants such as grasses and most catkins have their pollen-bearing stamens fully exposed on the outside rather than protected within, and they produce pollen in vast quantities to compensate for the hit-and-miss element of the process.

Pollination and seed setting may not be of great importance in the flower beds but for edible and ornamental fruit production they are essential. This is a sound reason, therefore, for planting such species as *Buddleia davidii*, thymes and *Sedum spectabile*: in attracting butterflies and other insects and enhancing the visual appeal of the summer garden, these plants help make it more productive too.

Flowering

Although leaves have an important (and often underrated) part to play in the ornamental garden, the vegetable plot is almost the last refuge of the flowerless garden plant. And even here, cauliflowers, broccoli and globe artichokes keep the floral flag flying. Almost wherever you look in the garden at this time of year, flowers fill your field of view. But why does an individual plant suddenly produce buds and ultimately flowers, rather than continuing to bear only leaves and shoots? The answers to this question cover some fascinating aspects of plant biology.

The reasons that determine whether a plant is an annual (which flowers in the same year that it germinated), biennial (flowers in the following year) or perennial (flowers, usually on a regular basis, for many years) are lost in the mists of evolutionary time. So, too, are the reasons why some plants – such as daffodils – produce their flowers singly, whereas others – delphiniums, for instance – develop huge spikes bearing masses of separate blossoms. But something must determine the moment when flowers form or the particular year that a plant blooms for the first time. And there must be a reason why the blooms are produced sparsely or prolifically. For these features cannot have a wholly evolutionary basis, being variable between individual plants. Can we as gardeners influence them?

In my discussion of plant feeding (see below), I mention one factor that certainly influences flower formation. The type of fertilizer or, more specifically, the balance of plant nutrients that the fertilizer contains, goes a long way towards dictating the relative effort that the

Two of the most popular border perennials give an indication of the variety of types of flower: oriental poppies have luscious large blooms, only one to a stem, delphiniums, in contrast, carry a multitude of small flowers on tall imposing spikes.

If the garden is to put on the best possible display of flowers, whether in the form of a cloud of catmint (*above*), or a pretty planting of foxgloves, *Alchemilla mollis*, saponaria, *Rosa mundi* and *Clematis* 'Nelly Moser' (*right*), the plants must be kept well fed throughout the summer.

plant puts into leaf, root and flower formation. A fertilizer containing a high proportion of potash in relation to nitrogen almost always encourages more flower development. If there is a reluctant flowerer among your perennials, or if you have a fast-growing plant such as a tomato and want the maximum number of fruits, apply a potash-rich feed. But such treatments are really to be thought of as fine-tuning the flowering phenomenon. The underlying causes of flower-bud initiation are the environmental variables, temperature and light. With many types of plant, a certain temperature must be attained (or not exceeded) for flowering to start. However, light is of even greater importance. And it is not light intensity that matters, it is day length.

Plants that originate naturally from regions relatively close to the South and North Poles are stimulated to flower by hormonal changes that occur when the days are fairly long: they are called long-day plants. Conversely, plants from closer to the Equator are stimulated by short days. In the garden, of course, we can't really do very much to influence day length, although in greenhouses it can be adjusted by the use of artificial lighting and periodic darkening so that the plants flower when the grower chooses. Hence pot chrysanthemums are available all year round whereas outdoors they only flower in the autumn.

Feeding Plants

Gardening writers are always advising along the lines of 'apply a base-dressing before planting and then give liquid feed regularly throughout the growing season'. Base-dressings, top-dressings and side-dressings are discussed elsewhere in the book, but liquid feeding has a more immediately topical significance. All of these instructions, however, carry the message that to grow, plants must be fed, and that in the height of summer they must be fed especially assiduously.

Plant feeding can be as simple or as complicated as the gardener chooses to make it. But there are certain essential nutrients that every

plant requires to achieve its real potential. During the summer, when growth is at its fastest, the naturally available supply of these essential nutrients is in the greatest danger of being exhausted.

Plants feed in two quite different ways. From the air, they absorb carbon dioxide and water, then combine these with the aid of chlorophyll in the process called photosynthesis. The end results are carbohydrates, which are used in part to add bulk to the plant and in part as an energy store that is released during respiration. There is no need to improve the supply of water and carbon dioxide: the air contains a never-ending source.

But we can do a great deal to influence the availability of the second type of nutrient, the mineral substances that plants derive from the soil. The most important of these are nitrogen, phosphate and potash – known in gardening shorthand as N, P and K. Again, in oversimplified but useful gardening shorthand, nitrogen promotes leafy growth, phosphate helps root development, and potash assists flower and fruit formation. A range of other nutrients are also essential but required in lesser amounts. Iron, calcium, magnesium and boron are among the most important of them. If plants are suffering from shortages of a particular type of food, it soon becomes obvious: for example, a shortage of iron results in the leaves turning pale yellow with conspicuous dark green veins.

Repeatedly growing the same plants on the same area of soil inevitably depletes the natural supply. It is up to you to replace the nutrients that have been used. Routine use of fertilizers is absolutely essential if plants are to give of their best. During the summer, when growth is proceeding apace, it is often simplest to use the liquid fertilizers mentioned earlier. There are two reasons for this: already being in solution, the active ingredient reaches its target more quickly; and because plants are able to absorb a small amount of liquid through their leaves, so a liquid fertilizer applied as a foliar feed offers the fastest method of all to deliver the goods to where they are needed.

The Unsung Virtues of Good Timing

In a gardener's experience few things compare with being able to step outside the kitchen door on a warm summer's morning and pick home-grown vegetables fresh from the garden. Rows of lettuces, carrots, herbs and beetroot are there for the taking. But the richness of the moment can turn to frustration when the rows turn from a sufficiency into a glut. And the frustration intensifies when, a few weeks later, the glut has been replaced with plants run to seed.

One of the most important but under-appreciated skills of gardening is to arrange for plants to mature at the time they are needed most: thus, to provide continuity not glut. Although this is most obvious in the vegetable and fruit gardens, it happens in the ornamental beds too where there can be periods of several weeks when all is a blaze of colour followed by others when there is only foliage to gladden the eye.

There are various tricks and devices that can be employed to spread the pleasures and fruits of our labours. Perhaps the simplest, certainly in the vegetable plot, is to sow sequentially. Most seed packets give instructions like 'sow outdoors from April to September', which means sow at regular intervals between the given months. In most instances, a small sowing every two weeks will suffice. This spread can be improved

A vegetable garden can become almost too much of a blessing if care is not taken to calculate how much of each crop is required at any one time. Sow small quantities of seed at intervals and plant varieties that mature at different times throughout the summer.

further by careful choice of varieties: with carrots for instance, choose an early, a mid-season, and a late or maincrop variety. Even if you restrict yourself to sowing directly in the garden, the season can be extended at both ends by using cloches, which give an earlier start to seedlings and enable crops to be kept in the ground at the end of the summer as the weather cools. And by raising at least some of the plants in the greenhouse or cold frame and then putting them out in the garden as transplants, you can steal a march on those sown directly.

With perennials – be they fruit trees and bushes, shrubs or herbaceous perennials – sowing times offer no flexibility. But the choice of species and varieties is of paramount importance. By selecting three types each of raspberry, strawberry and blackcurrant, for example, the length of the soft fruit season can be at least doubled. And by carefully examining the flowering times of ornamental plants *before* you buy them, you will be able to ensure interest all summer long.

55

Preparing for Drought

It is a paradox of the summer that the weather is rarely acceptable to the majority of people. Throughout the winter and the spring, we look forward to the long summer days and then complain whatever the weather. I have never worked out if it is too much or too little rain that causes a gardener the greatest anguish. And, of course, it is an ancient custom to complain that things have changed within our lifetimes, and that the summers are no longer as good as they used to be. Curiously, however, most weather is not as unpredictable as it might seem.

In most regions, a drought may be expected at least once a year (and, indeed, sometimes occurs in winter). Technically, a drought is simply a period of 15 days when no measurable rain has fallen, although a rather longer dry period than this is usual before restrictions on the use of water are imposed. But for many types of plants the consequences are fairly swift to appear. On the next page I discuss in more detail the functional needs that plants have for water; it is the absence of adequate supplies of moisture in the soil that is the feature of a drought and the aspect considered here.

The rain that falls on to the surface of the soil is lost in three main ways: some drains away into the sub-soil, thence into the underlying rocks and so into rivers and the sea; some evaporates from the surface layers of the soil before it has the chance to drain away at all, and some is taken up by plant roots, only to travel up through the stem to the foliage and then evaporate at the surface of their leaves. Little water drains away in a heavy soil, whereas in a light, sandy one too much is lost and, during a drought, it is the plants growing in the light, free-draining soil that usually suffer first and worst. Water is drawn from a soil with a high clay content only when the drought is prolonged, but when this does occur, of course, the whole sets like concrete and the consequences for plant life are very serious.

By improving soil structure through the incorporation of composts, manures or other forms of organic material, however, much of the potential damage from drought can be avoided. Much further benefit can be derived from regular mulching early in the year, while the soil is still moist. In itself, however, a mulch does not improve the moisture content of soil: there is no point mulching a dry soil because it will remain dry. But it is important to be prepared in advance and, by regular annual topping up both of organic matter dug into the soil and of mulch laid on top the summer will present your garden as an oasis of green while all around may be wilting.

The damp soil around the margins of a pond forms ideal conditions for many plants, including ferns, irises, candelabra primulas and giant cowslips (*Primula florindae*).

Water's Vital Role

In summer the garden pond literally hums with the busy activity of flying insects above the surface, while below, different types of insects and countless other forms of cold-blooded animal life are in states of heightened excitement as their bodies' metabolism rises in tune with the temperature. And from the mud in the bottom of the pool emerge water plants, also growing vigorously in the rather short season that an aquatic life affords. Only their flowers rise above the water's surface so pollination can take place. Although relatively few types of flowering plant have returned to what may well have been their ancestral aquatic home, such plants as *Myriophyllum* and *Elodea* nonetheless fill an essential role in supplying oxygen for the benefit of the fish and other inhabitants of the garden pond. Rather more species thrive in the permanently swampy conditions at the pond's edge, most notably the many types of bog primula.

But even those plants such as desert cacti that never see a pond or bog and seldom benefit from any rainfall have an important need for water. The entire bodily bulk of plants – all plants – is in fact very largely occupied by it. Plants' cells are filled with protoplasm, which is over 90 per cent water. More important still, it is the pressure exerted by the watery solutions of mineral salts within the cells that is responsible for the relative rigidity that plant tissues display. If you doubt the plausibility of this, compare a deflated rubber balloon with one filled with water in order to assess the structural stiffness that water can provide. Only when the bulk of a plant becomes truly massive does this system prove inadequate, and then the necessity for a more durable framework is met by woody tissues.

But water has another – vital – role to play. It is in a water solution that mineral nutrients are taken up from the soil and moved within the plant's cells. Indeed, all of the plant's biochemical functions are performed within such aqueous solutions. This is the reason why all fertilizers must be water soluble. And all pesticides and fungicides must be at least partly water soluble for them to be able to confer their protective benefits. Deprive a plant of water and you not only deny it its structural stability but also bring about its starvation and debilitation.

A Garden of Hybrids

Every garden worthy of the name is a blend of many and varied parts. Its physical shape and the way that the structural elements are put together is, of course, important. But it is the great diversity of the plant life that really gives it spice. I was once taken to task for saying that the modern garden is a garden of hybrids, but I stand by my assertion. Only in the hands of the devoted plantsman or woman will natural species predominate, even though quite a high proportion of shrubs and trees are unaltered from their natural state. The reasons for both of these facts are not difficult to see.

The hybrid plant is the same as the mongrel or cross-breed animal: the offspring of two unlike parents of different species or varieties. Generally, the hybrid is of greater vigour than its parents and this may be manifest in any number of appealing ways. The fruit or flowers may be larger, the leaves lusher, the growth faster. But the hybrid offers gardeners another great attribute too, for it combines some of the features of both parents. For example, with two species, one having large pink flowers and one with small red ones, we are given the chance, if we so wish, to have plants with flowers both large and red. Clearly, to produce a hybrid artificially, cross-pollination must be effected, seeds set and progeny raised. With an annual plant, this can take place within a single season; with a herbaceous perennial, within a few seasons. However, with shrubs and trees, the process can occupy almost a gardener's lifetime. Small wonder, therefore, that most of the hybrid trees grown in our gardens are the results of natural crossings.

Of course, not every crossing produces garden-worthy plants. A process of selection, of weeding out the less desirable individuals must take place; they, in turn, must be crossed again to strengthen the character or characters being selected. There is great skill in the

Among the most valuable of plants for summer colour in containers are hybrid pelargoniums. In mild areas, such varieties as this deep pink, ivy-leaved trailing form (*above*) can be allowed to grow outdoors permanently.

carefully directed crossings made by professional plant breeders, but every gardener can capitalize on crossings that occur naturally by collecting and growing-on self-sown seedlings found close to similar parental plants. And with a little time and effort, it is perfectly possible, provided certain simple precautions are taken to avoid self-pollination, to make your own crossings deliberately by transferring pollen from the stamens of one plant to the stigma of the other.

There is one important area of gardening, which is not actually visible to the gardener, where carefully bred and selected hybrids are used. Modern fruit trees are grown, not on their own roots, but grafted on to specially bred rootstock varieties. These rootstocks not only serve to replace the vigour that may have been lost during the repeated crossings and selections made for fruit quality – it is as easy to breed out features from a hybrid as it is to breed them in – but they also exercise an influence over the ultimate size of the tree. So the apple trees in the modern garden are not small through having been neglected, under-fed or over-pruned. Rather, they are small because the gardener has chosen an appropriate dwarfing rootstock to provide a tree commensurate with the dimensions of the garden.

Almost every plant in this lovely late-summer border is a hybrid – the phlox, day lilies, lilies, heleniums, achilleas and others have all been changed by careful breeding from their ancestors. In this way, we have plants with larger, more colourful flowers and with a longer blooming period.

'Constance Spry', a beautiful, vigorous modern shrub rose, can survive even in relatively poor conditions. But if it is not to succumb to the common pests and diseases that afflict even the toughest roses – such as aphid, black spot, mildew and rust – it must be planted in the best possible conditions and kept properly fed and watered through the summer.

Keeping the Garden free of Pests and Diseases

Nature is at her most bounteous in summer and surely all must be right with the world. Well, almost all right, for I can almost promise that if you take a slightly closer look at your plants, there will be the odd blemish or two here and there. Unfortunately, insects and other pests as well as disease-causing fungi, bacteria and viruses all find plants at least as appealing as we do, and every type of plant provides the staple diet of some creature or other.

But must this army of parasites be eradicated in the cause of better gardening? I believe that here, as with so much in life, moderation is a sound maxim to follow: even though there are a very few pests or diseases that, if allowed to continue unchecked, would certainly prevent the successful growing of individual types of plants, gardeners should exercise tolerance generally. There are several reasons for this. First, in most cases the damage caused is very slight and unlikely to be more than disfiguring: the supermarket greengrocery shelves have tricked us into believing that every fruit, vegetable and cut flower must be of production-line perfection. Second, only a small proportion of the wildlife of our gardens is in any way harmful, and measures taken to counteract this minority may well damage the innumerable beneficial creatures, many of which, if left to their own devices, keep pests and diseases down to manageable levels.

I have some simple guidelines for keeping the garden as healthy as possible and for ensuring that summer beds and borders stay lush and free from holes. Keeping the garden tidy is essential: many of the problem-causing creatures survive and proliferate on piles of old prunings, on dead flower heads left where thrown and on old leaves that have been allowed to accumulate. And growing plants in the recommended manner helps them to protect themselves from attack: grow them in the correct compost, at the optimum spacing, water and feed as appropriate to their requirements, prune when necessary, stake where relevant and they will be less prone to succumb to trouble.

If, despite your endeavours, a pest or disease does gain more than a foothold, some direct action is called for. The first should be purely physical: cutting away the damaged leaf, removing the individual affected plant or even picking off the pest itself. If these measures don't work, then you may have to use a chemical control, but here, exercise caution. Initially try safer, well-tried fungicides such as sulphur or Bordeaux mixture, or the non-persistent insecticides such as derris or pyrethrum. Alternatively, choose a modern selective substance such as the insecticide pirimicarb that kills aphids but leaves beneficial lacewings, hover-flies and ladybirds relatively untouched. I would always avoid using systemic insecticides (those that are absorbed into the plants' tissues) on any edible produce.

Ornamental cabbages suffer from the same pests and diseases as their less decorative relatives. To reduce the likelihood of problems, change the planting position of your cabbages every year and keep the vegetable garden free of all dead plants, rubbish and weeds. Keep the plants well-nourished and take action at the first sign of trouble.

PLANNING THE SUMMER GARDEN

As a key feature of the garden, a border requires careful planning, especially if it is to provide sustained colour and interest throughout the year. A mixed border of herbaceous and woody perennials, including hostas, roses, astilbes and *Alchemilla mollis*, has flowers and foliage to provide varied attractions, whatever the time of year.

Mixed and Herbaceous Borders

A 'true' herbaceous border is a dramatic phenomenon. Composed entirely of herbaceous perennials, it is a riot of colours that forms in summer (*right*) then dies back totally at the end of the season to lie dormant beneath a bare exterior (*below*).

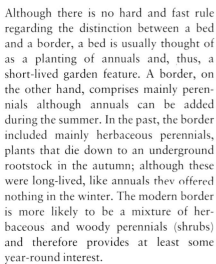

Winter

Summer

Although there is no hard and fast rule regarding the distinction between a bed and a border, a bed is usually thought of as a planting of annuals and, thus, a short-lived garden feature. A border, on the other hand, comprises mainly perennials although annuals can be added during the summer. In the past, the border included mainly herbaceous perennials, plants that die down to an underground rootstock in the autumn; although these were long-lived, like annuals they offered nothing in the winter. The modern border is more likely to be a mixture of herbaceous and woody perennials (shrubs) and therefore provides at least some year-round interest.

The word border implies that the whole must be placed at one side of the garden, of the lawn or some other structural feature. Certainly a vertical background is important. This may be provided by a wall, a fence or a hedge (although hedges draw water and nutrient from the soil to the detriment of the other plants). It is perfectly possible to have an 'island border', surrounded by grass, gravel or paving, with the plants arranged rather in the manner of two conventional borders back to back (although those that I see in gardens are generally too small).

If it is to function satisfactorily, a perennial border requires a little more advance planning than almost any other garden feature. The position of the border is important, although its dimensions are even more so. In order to grow most of the popular and traditional border plants, such as lupins, phlox, delphiniums and Michaelmas daisies, you should choose the sunniest possible site; relatively few herbaceous perennials thrive in the shade. (The shrub component is less of a problem in this respect because many species tolerate at least moderate shade.) But unless the border is an adequate length and depth, there will be insufficient room to include enough plants to give continuity of colour (or foliage, fruit and so on) for more than a couple of months. My own preference is for a depth from front to back of at least 2.5 m (8 ft) and preferably 3 m (10 ft). Conversely, if it is more than about 4.5 m (14½ ft) deep, it will be extremely difficult to attend to staking, dead heading and other routine tasks in the centre of the plot. The length of the border should be at least 5 m (16 ft).

Always bear in mind that the border *is* a perennial feature – its plants will be in position for many years (although not literally forever). Ideally therefore, the entire site should be thoroughly cleared of perennial weeds and double dug in advance – you will only again be able to incorporate organic matter at or below rooting depth when individual plants are replaced. Early autumn is the most suitable time to begin your preparation and you should scatter bone-meal as you work compost or well-rotted manure into the soil. It may well be difficult to complete

63

the planting in the autumn but this is no bad thing for it means that the slightly more tender plants and also evergreen shrubs (which suffer badly from cold winter winds when newly planted) can be left until the spring.

And so to the all-important matter of plant choice. There are so many different types of herbaceous perennial and ornamental shrub and so many different ideas on the colours that combine most attractively that I shall restrict myself to some general guidelines. But in all respects, I must urge you to do a little homework – use plant encyclopaedias, nursery catalogues and the labels on the plants themselves when you see them at the garden centre to inform yourself of their ultimate heights, spreads and flowering times. I have used previously the simile of a chessboard when planning a border and I think this does help for it conveys the impression of taller items at the back and in the centre with lower ones to the sides and in front. The king, queen and castles represent the basic shrubby framework and in the centre this role could be taken by tall shrubs, perhaps standards, or by a small tree. This should be a deciduous, light and open-structured tree however or it will cast too dense a shade for other plants nearby. The shrubs at the back corners (the 'castles'), should be lower-growing and here small-leaved evergreens work rather well, defining positive limits to the border in winter. Very small or dwarf shrubs are useful at the front of the border also – there is too often a tendency to rely here on low-growing or trailing herbaceous perennials, or even annuals, but the result is a very uninteresting appearance in winter. Low-growing, none too vigorous evergreens, especially such pale-leaved plants as lavender, are an ideal choice for creating some year-round interest in this prominent position at the front of the border.

Having chosen your shrubby framework, you will probably find this requires little further adjustment although some routine pruning may be necessary. But when you select the infilling herbaceous plants, you must be prepared for some

Colour is everything in this inspired combination of deep purple buddleia, pink *Lavatera olbia* and violet chicory (*left*). Height is also a factor, with the plants gradually ascending to the buddleia at the rear, an important consideration when planning your border.

A solid framework of well-chosen evergreen shrubs bordering a path (*below*) will guarantee winter interest as well as summer colour.

A composition in green and yellow forms the basis of this mixed border (*right*) with *Sambucus racemosa* 'Plumosa Aurea', yucca and *Alchemilla mollis*, whose green-yellow flowers will last until the middle of the season.

Alpine plants do not have to be restricted to a special garden (*below*). Ferns, small conifers and other alpines can be put to attractive use in a mixed border.

mistakes – we all make them. Perhaps the catalogue misled you and your chosen variety of lupin has finished flowering earlier than you expected, leaving a gap before the phlox behind it takes over later. Or possibly you were absolutely right in selecting for flowering time but underestimated the vigour of one of your plants and found its companions were swamped. Or again, perhaps choosing colours from someone else's descriptions resulted in a grouping of day lilies more akin to some medical complaint than anything of gardening appeal. Building up a border can be frustrating, occasionally disappointing, but for most of the time it is highly enjoyable and when, three or four years after you started, you have been able to correct your initial mistakes and it all works, the satisfaction is immense.

Glorious Bedding

Perhaps the most important, certainly the most characteristic, of the garden features that are peculiar to the summer months is the bed of annuals. Some are hardy, most are half hardy and many really are perennials when grown in their native warm climates; they are known collectively as bedding plants. The bed devoted solely to these plants is a typical, almost a diagnostic, feature of public parks and municipal gardens and it finds a place in many of the more formally organized home gardens. Even though a bed devoted entirely to such plants may be too overpowering for your tastes, they can play useful roles at the edges of herbaceous and mixed borders, as infilling between perennials of all types and in tubs, window boxes, hanging baskets and other containers.

The numbers of plants required for only a modest bedding scheme are considerable: even if you have a greenhouse and raise some of your own, you will almost certainly find it necessary to supplement these with plants bought at a garden centre or nursery. In order to obtain the best quality plants in the colours and varieties that you prefer, buy them around the middle of spring or order them in advance for collection at the beginning of

The essence of summer is evoked for some gardeners by the vibrant colours of bedding plants (*above*). Dramatic, densely-planted groups such as these begonias, demand large-scale planning, whether you are raising your own bedding plants from seed or tubers or buying them from a nursery.

One of the attractions of bedding plants lies in being able to plan a colour scheme and see it realized in such dramatic form only a few months later (*above right*). Swathes of colour are created here by the juxtaposition of nicotianas, marigolds and lavateras with handsome verbascums.

Lobelias, begonias and fuchsias (*below right*) cascade down a wall.

If you use plastic pots or troughs for plants inside a window box (*right*) you can replace them as necessary to have a changing, year-round display.

A real, or even reconstituted, stone urn (*below centre*) may seem an expensive purchase, but it will weather beautifully and is in fact a worthwhile investment.

summer. They may be planted out when the danger of frost has passed but do not assume that they have been hardened off; give the plants at least a week of protection in a cold frame.

There is great satisfaction to be derived from raising at least some of your own bedding plants from seed. Decide in advance which plants you require for your planting schemes. Before deciding which to raise and which to buy, check how long before planting out that each must be sown and the temperatures that each type requires for germination. This is important because there is little point in decid-

ing, for instance, that you will raise all your own pelargoniums if you do not have a propagator which can attain a temperature of at least 24°C (75°F) in late winter and an absolute minimum of 7°C (45°F) thereafter. Nor is there any merit in selecting types that all grow at a similar pace and therefore will put a strain on your germination, pricking on and hardening off facilities and time. Moreover, a few popular bedding plants, including salvias, fibrous-rooted begonias and petunias, have slightly special problems attached to their raising from seed that might lead to failure.

You can arrange bedding plants in the garden exactly as you choose. If the traditional colour combination of red salvias, blue lobelia and white alyssum appeals, then this is what you must have. If you are attracted by the carpet bedding so beloved of the Victorians, then choose low-growing, compact varieties: you can enjoy the hours with seed catalogues and plant descriptions trying to recreate a floral version of your favourite carpet, wallpaper or child's first picture. And don't neglect such plants as ornamental beetroot and sempervivums where the appeal and colour lie in the foliage.

The Rose Garden

Most gardeners have a soft spot for roses. And while there may be many, like me, who find it hard to embrace the whole of the vast rose tribe enthusiastically, there are species and varieties among the modern bushes, old shrubs, miniatures and climbers to suit all tastes. I have space only to offer some suggestions of the ways in which roses may be used and to indicate how they can be planned to fit into overall garden designs.

Although there is a popular belief that roses can only be grown satisfactorily in a clay soil, I know many gardens, including my own, that contradict this. Roses thrive in most soils, except possibly the very acidic or very alkaline, provided they are moisture retentive. Even acid soils can be helped by adding lime, and the annual use of a fertilizer containing sequestered iron ensures some success on a very chalky site. A clay provides moisture retentiveness naturally but a free-draining sandy loam or sand can be improved by digging in large quantities of organic matter thoroughly. And with all soils, the regular application of a surface mulch in autumn and again in spring helps to maintain the moisture-retaining structure (as well, of course, as suppressing weeds). Special care must be exercised if you plan to plant new roses on a site where roses have been grown previously for the soil may be infected by the mysterious rose sickness or rose replant disease. The main cause of this seems to be microscopic pathogenic soil fungi. The only ways to avoid its effects are by leaving about two years between removing the old plants and

Different varieties of shrub rose (*left*), including *Rosa alba*, grown together and among other herbaceous plants such as delphiniums result in a delightfully informal tangle of blooms.

introducing the new, or by removing a cube of soil with sides equal to about one and a half spade's depths at each planting position and filling the hole with fresh soil from another part of the garden on which roses have not been grown previously.

Free-standing roses, be they bushes, shrubs or miniatures, are usually grown massed together in beds. Such massed plantings dictate certain styles to the garden as a whole. You need only visit a municipal park to see the effect of a bed of modern large-flowered (hybrid tea) or

these very small forms because, with the few exceptions of those varieties that reach about 45 cm (18 in), they will be lost in a larger area. Even though such a bed will still be formal, its much more delicate nature and smaller size means that it will have less impact on the surrounding area. I find that a site close to the house, adjacent to a paved area and perhaps in a slightly raised bed, or even in large tubs standing on such an area, offers the best opportunity for the tiny blooms to be seen and appreciated.

used as individuals or in small groups within much larger planting schemes. I find that a group of three similar hybrid tea varieties or old shrubs blends splendidly in a mixed border where their uninspiring appearance when out of bloom is scarcely noticed. Try using the lower-growing shrubs, such as some of the smaller hybrid rugosas, within a herb garden for a really traditional feel to a planting. And don't forget that there are no rules that forbid you to mix ornamental and edible plants – I use a

In early summer the shrub rose 'Nevada' (*far left*) is a mass of creamy-white flowers, each with a central point of yellow stamens.

The delightful yellow flowers of the rose 'Canary Bird' (*left*) bloom very early in the season. The rose season is a long one and, with careful planning, your garden can enjoy a continuous display of rose blooms right through to winter.

cluster-flowered (floribunda) varieties: a fairly formal creation which imposes a formality on all around it. In such plantings, the more floriferous and continuously flowering cluster roses usually work better than the finer, but usually shorter blooming, large-flowered forms. And single colours generally create greater impact than mixtures. Perhaps the ideal place for this type of rose planting is a large garden or public park, where separate beds can be devoted to individual varieties and colours.

Devoting an entire bed to miniature roses is probably the best way of growing

A massed bed of shrub roses, be they the more familiar old varieties or modern shrubs, does not have the same formal feel as bush roses grouped together. This is largely because the plants themselves are not pruned with the same neat perfection – most are scarcely pruned at all – and the overall shapes both of plants and blooms are those of careless informality. In a mature bed of shrub roses, the plants may be allowed to grow together until the whole becomes a mass of foliage over which the voluptuous blooms of white, pink and red hang with timeless abandon.

Of course, all free-standing roses can be

weeping standard rose in the centre of a fairly formal bed of lettuces and find the effect charming.

The positioning of climbing roses, too, results in similar effects of formality and informality. The more rampant, less disciplined climbing forms of old shrubs or most of the climbing species are much better grown as they occur naturally – up and through old trees or over old buildings. On the other hand, the climbing forms of large-flowered and cluster-flowered roses can be trained on trellis against a house wall, pruned annually to ensure that they are kept within bounds.

Container Gardening

When planning the container garden there are three main factors to consider: the choice of containers and compost, the choice of plants, and the disposition and arrangement of them in the limited space you have available.

The choice of container – its type, size and shape – depends on cost and the type of house and garden that you have. Costs range from the extremely cheap moulded plastic through concrete and wood to machine-made and then hand-thrown terracotta and fine quality reconstituted stone. The most expensive – and beautiful – of all are made of real antique stone or lead. Plastic containers are useful and inexpensive, but they are only ever imitations of something better and always appear so. In addition, they deteriorate in time, do not mellow attractively and have the functional disadvantage of permitting the compost within to become waterlogged. Because they are non-porous, it is difficult for gaseous exchange between compost and outside air to take place. It makes sense, therefore, to replace plastic containers as finances permit.

The choice between stone or concrete, on the one hand, and terracotta on the other should be dictated to some extent by the construction of your house – red brick houses, for instance, usually appear best when embellished with reddish terracotta. If you plan to leave the containers outside all year round, choose a terracotta that is frost resistant (most Spanish and Italian types are not). And be aware that some new concrete containers contain residues of setting agents that may be toxic to plants; they will only function efficiently when well weathered. The weathering process itself – of stone, concrete or terracotta – can be helped along by painting milk or liquid cow manure on the surface to encourage the growth of mosses, algae and lichens. The style and patterning of the containers is a matter of personal taste, but it's worth remembering that many of the patterns offered are based on those of much larger originals which look splendid outside stately homes but faintly ridiculous when scaled down to domestic proportions.

Your choice of container is at least as important as the plant you choose to put in it, especially if they are to be the centrepiece of an area. The rounded shape of *Anthemis cupaniana* (*above*) complements that of the stone urn beautifully and is echoed in the grasses growing close to its base.

Hanging baskets (*above*) can transform the barest of walls and are really invaluable for providing dramatic summer colour, particularly in urban settings.

When choosing hanging baskets, avoid those that are shallow and broad (saucer-shaped): these hold little compost and dry out very swiftly. Bowl or even cup-shaped baskets are much better. And do be certain that the hanging brackets are adequately anchored. For window boxes, much the best plan is to make wooden boxes with drainage holes, to the shape and size of the window ledge. Line these with plastic sheet and place individual plastic pots or troughs containing the plants inside the boxes – this is a flexible option, allowing you to change the scheme whenever you wish or to replace worn-out plants during the summer.

It is important to choose a good growing medium or compost. Large containers with large, long-term hardy plants are best filled with John Innes No 3 soil-based potting compost. With smaller pots and hanging baskets (where weight is an important consideration) it is better to use a peat-based medium. If you intend to grow lime-hating plants such as camellias or rhododendrons, use an ericaceous compost, which lacks lime.

Very few plants do not thrive in containers – even fruit trees can be successfully grown in wooden half-barrel tubs. Generally, summer colour will be provided by half-hardy annuals, perhaps using as a centrepiece a larger plant such as a specimen pelargonium or a fuchsia that has been overwintered under protection. And for the early part of the summer, lilies make splendid subjects.

I find that the impact of plants in containers is greatest when the containers are grouped – for example, three or four pots containing a selection of herbs and a specimen lavender or rosemary placed on one part of a paved area with a group of fuchsias (including one standard) in another. Single containers at corners or on steps break up the angularity of a sharp edge. The possibilities are endless – and endlessly pleasing too.

Container plants can be subtly integrated into the garden itself (*below*). All petunias have a long flowering period which will last right through to the end of the season, provided they are dead headed regularly.

An arrangement of containers can transform any paved area (*above*). The grand urn overflowing with ivy is probably more suitable for the larger garden, but the clipped bay tree and trained box could usefully decorate the smallest town garden patio.

Lilies in simple terracotta pots (*right*) provide early summer colour and a delightful scent to enhance any sitting area.

71

Climbing Plants for Summer

Many varieties of the climbing plants – roses and clematis, for instance – that I eulogized over for the spring garden will, of course, provide colour and interest right through the summer also. To their number may be added a few more climbers and wall shrubs that enhance the summer months.

One of the most useful is the deciduous, self-clinging climbing *Hydrangea petiolaris*, which bears white flowers against a background of fresh green, rounded leaves from mid summer onwards and is a particularly valuable plant for a shady wall. And every garden needs the white summer *Jasminum officinale*, a plant that requires warmth and sunshine and which rewards you with a heavenly perfume. The blooms of the passion flower, at once beautiful and dramatic, are always at their best in a warm sheltered position; the commonest species, *Passiflora caerulea*, is robust enough to produce vigorous new growth even after its top is killed back in a hard winter. The so-called potato vine, *Solanum crispum*, has a long flowering season (particularly so in the variety 'Glasnevin') and will decorate a warm wall with its purple, potato-like flowers all through summer.

Often neglected for summer appeal are several species of hardy and half-hardy annual and hardy herbaceous climbers. Most of the former are best raised from seed sown in pots in the protection of a greenhouse in early spring, and then hardened off and planted out when the danger of frost has passed, much as you would raise bedding plants. The tropaeolums form a useful group of vigorous red-, orange- or yellow-flowered climbers. The most familiar is the climbing nasturtium, *Tropaeolum majus*, which is so fast

Climbing plants are invaluable in an area of limited size, where verticals must be exploited to the full. A rose trained around an arch and the early-summer flowering clematis 'Nellie Moser' trained up a wall can transform the smallest of paved areas.

growing that it can actually be sown directly outdoors. Choose a warm, sunny spot with the poorest soil in your garden and you will have an abundance of blooms (that are edible and look beautiful in summer salads). *T. speciosum* is really a perennial and hardy enough to be left outdoors to overwinter as a rootstock after its top dies back. It looks at its best growing through an evergreen hedge. The bright yellow-flowered *T. peregrinum*, the canary creeper, is invaluable when grown as an annual either in pots with tall cane or stick supports or when allowed to trail down from hanging baskets.

Thunbergia alata, the black-eyed Susan, has orange-yellow, dark-centred flowers and is more restrained than the tropaeolums – a particular advantage in smaller containers in smaller gardens. *Cobaea scandens*, the cup and saucer vine, is a useful 2 to 3 m (6½ to 9 ft) tall climber with violet-petalled flowers surrounded by a conspicuous calyx; grow it as a half-hardy annual. The glory vine, *Eccremocarpus scaber*, is a scrambling climber, lovely entwined in old trees with its masses of small orange-red, nodding flowers. Although it will die back to a rootstock and sprout anew each year, the

plants seem short-lived and are best raised from seed as half-hardy annuals.

Finally, we must not forget the sweetest scented, easiest and most rewarding of all hardy annual climbers, the sweet pea. For the best results sow the seeds indoors in autumn or spring and then harden off the plants before putting them out, although you can also obtain good results by sowing the seed directly. Choose between the more formal support of bamboo canes or the informality of a wigwam of tall twigs. But remember to keep cutting the flowers, because once they begin to form seed, flower production declines.

Hydrangea petiolaris (left) tolerates shade well, is self-clinging – yet causes no damage to the structure it climbs – and carries delicate white flower clusters from mid season onwards.

Clematis jackmanii (above) is understandably one of the most popular varieties of clematis and its stunning purple flowers may continue through to the end of the season.

The Herb Garden

A bouquet of fresh herbs conjures up good, tasty home-made food. Fresh herbs are a far cry from the packets of green sawdust that masquerade as the dried equivalent. No cook, no gardener, can have any excuse for not growing herbs. They are extremely easy to cultivate, they are small and even a fairly extensive planting takes up no more than a couple of square metres (yards). You don't even need a garden at all as almost all herbs can be grown in containers.

It's useful to think of the herb garden as a short-term mixed border, mainly populated with small perennial shrubs, but with some herbaceous species and a few annuals too. My short list of herb-garden essentials includes at least one variety each of mint, thyme, sage, chives, marjoram, French tarragon, rosemary and bay among the perennials, together with basil and parsley which are grown as annual and biennial respectively. The most difficult choices are mint and thyme, which both have many different varieties; apple mint and one of the bushy silver-foliaged thymes, such as 'Silver Posie', would be my preferences. Hopefully you will be able to find space for more than the basics I have listed and include a wide range of herbs, both for culinary and ornamental appeal. A visit to a good garden centre, or better still to one of the many specialist herb nurseries, will reveal the vast number now on offer.

Although most herbs originate from warm, dry climates and really need a well-drained sunny position, mint is moderately shade tolerant – I grow mine beneath the shade of a large bay bush at the back of the herb garden. Mint requires slightly special treatment for another reason, too. It is highly invasive and much the simplest way to contain it is to grow each plant in a 20 cm (8 in) diameter plastic pot, sunk to its rim in the soil. At the end of each season, lift the pot from the ground and trim away any roots or runners that emerge from the base or threaten to escape over the sides.

I call the herb garden a short-lived feature because most of the perennials decline in appearance and effectiveness after about three years. They should be renewed then, with fresh plants from a garden centre or nursery, or from cuttings taken in the summer of the second year ready for planting out at the beginning of the third. Basil should be raised afresh from seed each spring; as it is only half-hardy, sow it in pots in the green-

house and plant it out after the danger of frost has passed. Parsley should be sown directly outdoors in spring and again in autumn, giving cloche protection to the young plants through the winter. Some gardeners have difficulty in growing parsley and certainly its seed is always slow to germinate. If you have this problem, try dusting a little garden lime along the seed drill or, if this fails, sow small groups of seeds in pots of John Innes seedling compost in a greenhouse and plant them out when they are well established. It is often suggested that mature parsley (as opposed to young plants) can only remain green and fresh over winter in cloches, but I have found it survives perfectly well without protection in a reasonably sheltered border, even in fairly cold areas.

The style of the herb garden can be informal or formal. Most formal herb gardens derive their patterning from the regular knot gardens and other geometric features of Tudor or earlier gardens. The only thing to remember when laying out an informal garden is that you need easy access to all parts of it to collect herbs for use, and whichever herb garden style you prefer, bear in mind that it should be close to the kitchen. Even the most devoted

A herb garden can, and should, be visually attractive as well as functional (*left*). Conveniently sited close to the door and charmingly bordered by a low box hedge, this herb garden contains pink-flowered chives, bright green-leaved lemon balm and tall-growing lovage.

Herbs can also be grown in a more formal arrangement (*right*). This knot of box is based on the patterning of traditional Tudor herb gardens.

cook is unlikely to want to walk to the far end of the garden every time a sprig of mint is needed.

This is why growing herbs in containers is not restricted to gardeners with little or no garden. Containers can be moved around freely and the entire herb collection rearranged. Moreover, container-grown bay trees can be moved under cover or into a sheltered corner when cold weather threatens – frost and biting winds are the enemies of this delightfully fragrant plant. Mention of bay serves as a reminder that herbs should be thought of as much as ornamentals as edible plants. Not only are many extremely attractive in their own right but they combine wonderfully with other ornamentals; one of my favourite combinations is of the old, low-growing deep red shrub rose 'Tuscany Superb' surrounded with fennel, lavender and parsley.

One of the most popular designs for a herb garden takes the form of a cartwheel. In some instances a real cartwheel is laid on the ground (*right*) and herbs are then planted in the spaces between the spokes.

Basil
Sage
Rosemary
Fennel
Mint
Parsley
Thyme
Chives

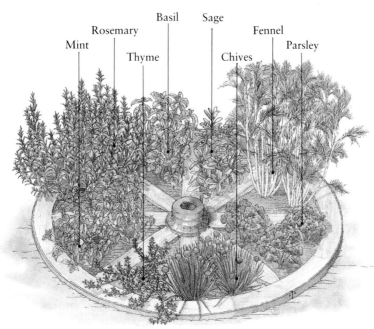

Herbs are just as successful grown informally alongside other plants (*above*). The only general point to bear in mind when considering the siting of herbs is easy access – you will want to get to the plants frequently so a position close to the house and perhaps adjacent to a path is ideal.

Soft Fruit

Whether it rains or shines, once the first strawberry has been eaten with thick cream, there can be no doubt that summer is here again. But strawberries are just a very small part of a succulent bounty that the soft-fruit garden can offer; and indeed, horticulturally, they are rather out on a limb from the rest. Despite the large range of plant types, soft fruit falls rather neatly into distinct groups, of which strawberries – low-growing and short-lived (four years at the most) – are one. The second group comprises the stiff-caned raspberries and their flexible, caned relatives – blackberries, loganberries, tayberries – and a few other less common fruits. The third group includes red and white currants and gooseberries, all grown equally easily as bushes or cordons. Blackcurrants, which superficially are similar to their red and white counterparts but culturally quite distinct and always grown as bushes, make up the fourth group.

Nonetheless, all soft fruit share certain requirements. They need as much sunshine as possible, a rich yet freely draining soil and almost invariably some protection from birds (which eat buds in winter and fruit in summer with equal relish). Given a suitable site, the necessary protection can be provided by throwing light-weight netting over the plants but purpose-made fruit cages are so easy to use that I would urge you to consider this seriously. A cage can be home-built from posts and lightweight netting although aluminium framed cages can be purchased relatively inexpensively. Although, of course, strawberries can be grown in a cage, they tend to take up a disproportionately large area of ground and need an unnecessarily large cage. My advice is to plant the strawberries separately (perhaps in the vegetable garden) and provide protection from birds with a simple netting cover or with cloches (which offer the additional advantage of an earlier crop).

A soft-fruit cage of about 36 sq m (43 sq yd) provides sufficient fruit for an average family to eat fresh during the summer, with ample left to freeze for the remainder of the year. In such a cage, you could grow, say, one and a half rows of raspberries (to include early, mid season and late varieties), two double cordons each of red and white currants and gooseberries, two early- and two later-maturing blackcurrants, plus three or four flexible caned fruit plants. The complementary strawberry bed will occupy an additional 5 to 6 sq m (6 to 7 sq yd).

As with all other perennial plants, thorough preparation of the soil within the fruit cage repays dividends, although if compost and manure are limited it is unnecessary to cultivate the entire area. Instead, thoroughly dig and fork in organic matter to at least 30 cm (12 in) depth in planting positions about 45 cm (18 in) diameter for those plants such as the blackcurrants that will be spaced widely apart. For cordon fruits and rows of canes, prepare a trench about 45 cm (18 in) wide and 30 cm (12 in) deep.

Autumn is the best time for planting all soft fruit bushes and canes. It is essential to obtain high-quality plants, certified to have been raised from virus-free stock. Very probably, you will find it worth-

while to order the plants well in advance because quantities of the newest varieties may well be limited. In general, soft fruit should be planted in much the same way as other shrubs, to about 1 cm (½ in) above the soil mark on the base of the stem. With raspberry canes, however, the uppermost roots should not be more than about 8 cm (3 in) deep, otherwise new cane development tends to be suppressed. Blackcurrants require special care, too, for they produce new shoots from the very base of the stem, and to encourage this they should be planted *deeper* than other plants; deeper, therefore, than the soil mark at the base of the stem.

It is even more important with strawberries than with other soft fruit to order plants in advance; order the largest container-raised plants on offer for early autumn delivery. Although you will find plants raised from cold-stored runners on offer at other times of the year, I have never found these as successful.

The strawberry bed should be prepared in much the same way as the vegetable bed. In many respects I think it helps to think of strawberries as vegetables rather

The vibrant colour of red currants and its promise of delicious fruit is as appealing to birds as to the gardener (*left*). The task of protecting soft fruit is made much easier if you build, or buy, a simple fruit cage.

Poppies add a bright splash of colour to the functional greens of raspberries and potato plants (*right*).

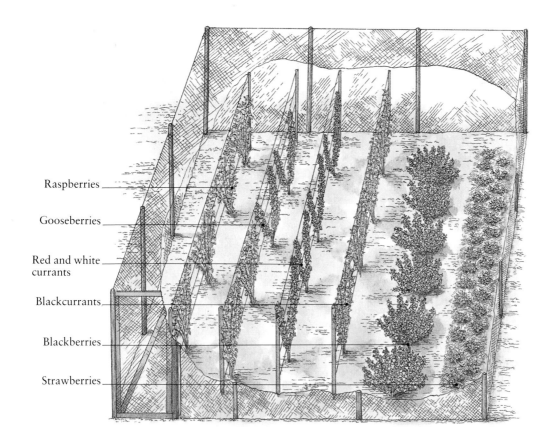

A soft fruit cage of about 42 sq m (50 sq yd) should provide fresh fruit throughout the season for the average family, with enough left over to freeze. Strawberry beds take up a relatively large area so if space in the fruit cage is a problem, plant them separately.

Raspberries

Gooseberries

Red and white currants

Blackcurrants

Blackberries

Strawberries

than fruit. The older varieties are best grown as annuals and even modern, high-yielding types, free from virus, should be replaced every three or four years. The most frustrating problems arise if the bed contains perennial weeds; I always take extra care to remove all traces of couch and similar problems. Of course, if you are using part of the vegetable plot, the land will have been regularly cultivated and, therefore, should be free from perennial weeds. It makes sound sense to rotate the strawberry bed much as you rotate the positioning of vegetables: strawberries are prone to virus problems which may persist in the soil. Although new stock will be virus-free, if there is a residue of contamination in the soil, the plants will rapidly become re-infected. Ideally, all new soft fruit canes and bushes should also be planted on a fresh site for the same reason. While this is rarely feasible, changing the positions of the different plants within the fruit cage may help.

Summer Vegetables

If space for a summer vegetable garden is limited, only plant the vegetables that are especially good when picked fresh rather than from the supermarket shelf, as well as those that are relatively expensive to buy. And it is worth planning carefully to ensure that the crops mature in sequence through the season and do not all produce an unmanageable glut.

Of the plants that began cropping in the spring, space should be allowed for further sowings of lettuce, spinach and spring onions (scallions) in the early part of the summer; these will mature as the season progresses. The most important of the slightly slower-growing types that only begin to yield in summer itself are radishes, beetroot, carrots and new potatoes, beans, the cucumber family, tomatoes and sweet corn.

Radishes are the easiest of all vegetables to grow. They thrive in all types of soil but grow best in a sunny position on a well-drained site. Allow space for rows about 2 m (6½ ft) long, to be sown approximately every three weeks from early spring to mid summer. If they are sown later than this, summer radish varieties are likely to bolt. Sow sparingly and thin later to leave about 2 cm (1 in) between plants. Radishes are very useful plants for intercropping between rows of slower-growing vegetables; as they grow so very quickly, they may also be catch-cropped – sown in any convenient space made vacant when other plants are removed. Both round- and long-rooted varieties are available, the round tending to be slightly earlier. 'Scarlet Globe' is perhaps the best round type, with 'French Breakfast' and 'White Icicle' the most reliable and tasty long-rooted forms.

The best summer beetroot are globes such as 'Crimson Globe' and 'Boltardy'. They require similar soil and site conditions to radishes. Calculate overall requirements (a row of 1 m [3 ft] should yield about 2 kg [4½ lb] of roots) and then sow in rows 30 cm (12 in) apart at monthly intervals from early spring to mid summer; the beetroot will attain their harvesting size (roughly the diameter of tennis balls) in two to three months.

The vegetable garden (*above* and *left*) is an area where forward planning and calculations are particularly well repaid. Annual crop rotation, speed of growth and cropping times, tolerance of shade and realistic supply of crop requirements for the size of your family are all factors to be carefully considered.

For carrots the soil must be free-draining, free from clods or hard, pan-like layers and contain no fresh manure (although well-rotted organic matter dug in a few months previously is extremely beneficial). The early-summer, quicker-growing varieties such as 'Early Nantes' or the round 'Early French Frame' yield about 2 kg (4½ lb) per m (3 ft); the later summer varieties such as 'Chantenay Red Cored' or 'Autumn King', slightly more. After calculating your requirements, sow seed of the early varieties in rows approximately 20 cm (8 in) apart at three-week intervals from early to mid spring, and then change to intermediate and maincrop types until mid summer.

To supply all of your potato requirements – say 2 kg (4½ lb) per week, either fresh or stored, throughout the year, you will need about 20 sq m (24 sq yd), which is the area of many people's entire vegetable plots. My advice is to concentrate on

new potatoes, which begin to crop in the first half of summer. (Although I should add that a crop of maincrop potatoes is very useful for clearing the ground in the first year on a new site because their dense leaf cover suppresses weeds very effectively.) Potatoes can be grown on most soils but they always benefit from thorough digging and manuring in the previous autumn and are likely to have their growth checked in cold, frosty positions. The yield of the early varieties grown as 'new' potatoes is less than that of the maincrop – expect about 1.5 kg per m (3⅓ lb per yd). Although the tubers are not planted until mid spring, it is a good idea to order your stock at the end of the previous winter and place them on trays in a light, frost-free position to induce them to sprout or 'chit'.

Runner beans begin to crop at the end of summer. They are best grown on a warm, sheltered site that has been deeply

79

Although runner beans (*right* and *below*) require supports at least 2 m (6½ ft) tall, they are an excellent vegetable to grow in a restricted space as they will give a high yield from a small area.

dug (trenched) and manured in the previous autumn. As they grow vertically (you must provide canes or sticks at least 2 m [6½ ft] tall for support), they give high yields from a small area: a 5 m (16 ft) double row should produce over 30 kg (67 lb) of beans. They may be raised from seed sown directly outdoors at the end of spring, although if you have a greenhouse and cold frame or other protected space, you will obtain earlier crops and generally more reliable plants by sowing the seed in 9 cm (3 ½ in) diameter pots in mid spring for transplanting outdoors once the danger of frost has passed. Choose between the older, generally more tasty, string varieties or the modern stringless forms.

French or dwarf beans require conditions similar to runner beans and can also be transplanted or sown directly at the same times. Their advantages are that they crop around one month earlier and they require no support. As they are bush plants rather than climbers, the yield is much lower: less than half that of runners.

Cucumbers, courgettes (zucchini) and marrows may be sown directly outdoors but are much more reliably raised from plants grown in the greenhouse from mid spring sowings in 9 cm (3½ in) pots, then planted outside after the danger of frost has passed. Both need very well-manured soil and can even be grown directly on a heap of compost. Cucumbers may be

Courgettes (*above*) are sprawling plants which demand an area of about 1.5 sq m (1⅘ sq yd) for six plants, which will supply the average family's needs.

Access is a consideration to bear in mind when planning your vegetable garden (*above right*). Space taken up by paths is worth sacrificing if damage to plants is thereby avoided and the task of tending them is made easier.

allowed to sprawl over the soil or can be trained up canes or other supports to save space. They are high-yielding and two plants will be ample for most family's requirements, giving one fruit each per week through the cropping period in late summer. Courgettes, even the so-called bush varieties, are fairly sprawling and you will require about six plants, occupying an area of around 1.5 sq m (1⅘ sq yd). Their relatives, melons, are grown in a similar manner but must have the protection of a cold frame or cloches. And the yield is small – you should not expect more than three or four fruits per plant.

Unless you live in a very mild area, outdoor tomatoes will not mature before the very end of summer and, therefore, I tend to think of them as autumn crops (see page 114). To grow summer tomatoes, you will need an unheated greenhouse. For most family's needs, eight plants will suffice. They will begin to crop in a 2 m by 2.5 m (6½ ft by 8 ft) greenhouse in one to two months after the last frosts. The seeds should be sown about 13 weeks before the last frost is expected; place the plants into their growing positions when they are nine weeks old. But bear in mind that there will be no room for any other plants in your greenhouse during this period; if this is unacceptable, you must reduce the number of plants – or buy a larger greenhouse. Much the best and easiest method of growing the plants is by ring culture (see Spring Tasks 12). As a change from the normal round red tomatoes, plan for a selection that also includes the sweet, small-fruited, the yellow-fruited and the large beefsteak varieties.

Sweet corn plants are large and are only worth growing if you live in an area with warm summers, have a light, fertile soil and plenty of room: on average, you will only obtain one to one-and-a-half cobs per plant and they really must be grown in blocks of ten or more for satisfactory pollination. Ten plants will occupy about 6 sq m (7 sq yd). Sow the seed in the greenhouse in mid spring and plant out after the danger of frost has passed.

SUMMER TASKS

1 A broad sweep of beautifully-kept lawn evokes the essence of a summer's day and needs little further adornment – only a sundial, perhaps, to provide an arresting feature in the expanse of green.

1 Lawns: maintenance

Lower the blade setting slightly on the lawn mower as the season begins and dry weather becomes regular. But never set it at its minimum value for this shaves the turf and encourages moss growth and other problems.

If the weather is dry for long periods, use a lawn sprinkler regularly. But if the water supply is restricted, use it where it is of greater value: in the vegetable and fruit gardens. It takes a very prolonged drought to damage turf permanently.

2 Weeds: applying weedkillers

During warm weather, continue to apply weedkillers to the garden where you have problems that cannot be controlled by weeding. But always be sure that you are using each product strictly as the manufacturer directs. When using a lawn weedkiller, allow three to four days after mowing before applying the chemical, and a further three to four days before mowing again.

3 Weeds: hoeing

During dry weather, use a Dutch or similar hoe among vegetable and ornamental beds to control annual weeds. Do not hoe close to soft fruit bushes and canes or onions, which have shallow root systems prone to damage.

4 Pests and diseases: controlling

Keep a continuing check on all plants for outbreaks of pests or diseases. Most are unlikely to require chemical control: odd leaves or shoot tips bearing aphids or caterpillars should be nipped off by hand. When a pest outbreak is more severe, use a contact rather than a systemic insecticide, especially on edible crops, whenever possible. Relatively minor diseases, such as those appearing as isolated leaf lesions, can often be checked by pulling off the affected parts. But more extensive attacks should be combatted by a systemic fungicide (in general, fungicides are much less environmentally harmful or toxic than insecticides).

Greenhouse

5   Ventilation

Open ventilators every day as the weather warms up. On hot days, open the door also. Severe harm could result from inadequate ventilation during very hot periods in the middle of the day.

6   Heating

Thermostatically controlled greenhouse heaters may be left switched on to prevent any damage arising from a sudden, very cold night at the start of the season. Most electric heaters can also be used as cooling fans, which are useful if switched on occasionally to prevent the air stagnating in very hot weather.

7   Feeding and watering

Feed and water all indoor plants regularly. If you have large numbers of pot plants, use capillary matting, ideally with clay pots where there is good contact between pot base and matting.

8   Aphids

Look carefully for the first signs of aphid infestation on tomatoes and other plants. The odd affected leaf should be picked off and destroyed; combat larger infestations with an insecticide 'smoke'.

9   White-fly attack

Look carefully for the first signs of white-fly attack by checking the undersides of the leaves where the insects congregate. Repeated use of a fumigant or very fine spray insecticide may check an attack. In a large greenhouse, however, it would be worth trying to control the pest biologically using the white-fly predator insect, *Encarsia*; if you do adopt this approach, you cannot then use insecticides to control other pests.

10   Red-spider mite

Look carefully for the first signs of red-spider mite infestation: mottling on the leaves and cobwebs on the foliage. The mites themselves are inconspicuous, only about 0.5 mm (¹/₅₀ in) long and dull orange in colour. Insecticides are of little value in controlling mites but regular misting with water and good ventilation help prevent the buildup of the hot, dry conditions that they prefer. In a large greenhouse, however, it is worth trying to control them biologically using the red-spider mite parasite, *Phytoseiulus*. Once the parasite has done its work fresh cultures must be used if there is a re-infestation.

11   Annuals: hardening off

As soon as the danger of frost has passed, half-hardy annuals raised from seeds or cuttings and large stock plants overwintered under cover should be taken outdoors. Plant them out after about a week or ten days of hardening off.

7 Capillary matting, with a reservoir of water and wicks made from strips of matting, ensures a constant water supply to the plants placed on it and has obvious advantages if you cannot be there for a time to water the plants. It is most effective with clay pots as plastic pots are not only lighter but usually have an indented base which does not encourage water uptake. If using capillary matting, water the plants with a can in the conventional way approximately once every two weeks in order to flush through accumulated salts from liquid fertilizers.

7 In a large greenhouse with a very large number of plants, (and a mains water supply nearby), it may be worth investing in a trickle irrigation system. Never add fertilizer to the water reservoir as this encourages algal growth and blocks the trickle nozzles.

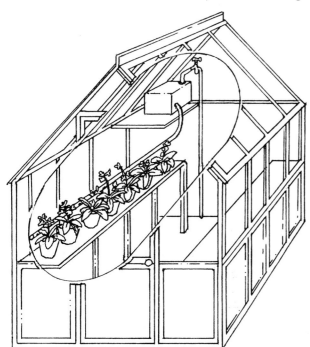

12 Perennials: re-potting

Complete the re-potting of house and greenhouse perennials, then move the more robust types into the garden for the summer. Azaleas, in particular, benefit from being placed in a warm, sheltered corner of the garden, preferably in a peat bed, with the pot sunk to its rim. Apply a liquid fertilizer every two or three weeks.

13 Tomatoes: care

Continue to tie in and side-shoot tomatoes regularly and feed once a week. Do not allow the compost or bed to dry out as this can lead to the disfiguring blossom end rot problem.

14 Vegetables and ornamental plants: sowing

Complete the sowing of vegetable and ornamental seeds, although with tomatoes and other crops taking up greenhouse space sowing directly into the garden may now be preferable.

15 Seedlings: pricking on

Prick on seedlings promptly and move them to a cold frame or another area outside which is partially sheltered from the sun.

16 Grapevines: care

Continue to tie in and stop side-shoots on grapevines. As soon as the fruit is set, thin them out to approximately half with a pair of blunt scissors. Check for signs of mildew or grey mould; spray with systemic fungicide if necessary.

17 Chrysanthemums: cuttings

At the start of the season take cuttings of the mid- and late-season types of indoor chrysanthemums; these can be planted in large pots or directly into greenhouse soil borders approximately six weeks later. Move potted mature plants of greenhouse varieties to an outdoor standing area.

18 Carnations and pinks: cuttings

In mid season, take cuttings approximately 5 cm (2 in) long from non-flowering shoots of outdoor carnations and pinks. Dip them in hormone rooting powder and strike them in the greenhouse in the normal peat-and-sand medium (made up of equal parts, by volume) in a propagator.

19 House plants: sowing

Around mid season, sow seeds of house plants such as cyclamen for flowering next year. Prick the seedlings into individual 8.75 cm (3½ in) pots when they are 2 to 3 cm (1 to 1¼ in) tall.

20 Pelargoniums: cuttings

At the end of the season, take cuttings of pelargoniums for overwintering; but only do so if you have sufficient space to keep them in their pots over winter.

21 Winter lettuces: sowing

At the end of the season, sow winter lettuces in individual pots for transplanting later to greenhouse borders or growing bags (spring varieties for planting outdoors are sown later under cloches; see **79**).

22 Perennial ornamentals: sowing

At the end of the season, sow seeds of perennial ornamentals for pricking on later into pots and overwintering in a cold frame. But bear in mind that many of the best named varieties of popular cultivated types must be propagated by cuttings.

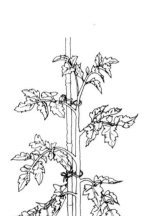

13 During the summer months tying the stems of tomatoes in to canes will probably have to be done at least once a week. Ensure the string is not too tight.

13 Side-shooting is essential to create a productive tomato plant and you may need to do this daily. Pinch out side-shoots growing in leaf axils when they are 2.5 cm (1 in) long.

18 1. Choose a strong side-shoot on the carnation with four or five pairs of developed leaves and remove the lower pair. Dip in hormone rooting powder or in water first if the powder will not adhere.

2. Use the normal peat-and-sand mixture in a covered propagator. Make planting holes and push in the cuttings up to the base of the leaves. Rooting should then take place in two to four weeks.

Trees and Shrubs

23 Trees and shrubs: cuttings

At the end of the season, take semi-hardwood cuttings from trees and shrubs. Strike them in the normal way in a peat-and-sand medium in a covered propagator (see **18**).

24 Roses: care

To produce the best flowers on bush roses, especially on large-flowered types (hybrid teas), prune off side-shoots bearing flower buds. This allows the plant to concentrate its resources in the single bloom at the shoot tip.

Spray all roses every three weeks with a fungicide and insecticide mixture to combat mildew, black spot and aphids.

As soon as the first flush of rose flowers has begun to fade, dead head the plants. Cut stems bearing the dead flower heads back to the first leaf with five (not three) leaflets that adjoins an outward-facing bud. After this first flowering, give the plants a top-dressing with a proprietary rose fertilizer to encourage a further blooming in autumn.

25 Trees: staking

Check the ties on staked trees: with growth taking place rapidly, stems can quickly become constricted if the ties are too tight.

26 Heather: cuttings

Around mid season, take cuttings from heather plants. Pull away young shoots and root them in the usual way in a peat-and-sand medium in a covered propagator (see **18**) in a sheltered place, out of direct sunlight.

27 Evergreens: pegging down

Peg down low-growing branches of evergreens and other plants that root with difficulty from cuttings to produce layers. It is

24 Large-flowered roses often develop side-shoots with flower buds as well as the main bud at the tip. Remove these side-buds to enhance the quality of the main bloom.

24 On hybrid teas cut back stems with dead flower heads to above the first leaf with five leaflets which adjoins an outward-facing bud.

28 Common early-summer-flowering shrubs that require routine pruning:

Abutilon vitifolium Lightly shorten the longest shoots only after flowering.
Buddleia alternifolia Shorten old flowered shoots only after flowering.
Clematis (large-flowered hybrids) Cut back lightly in late winter to strong new buds, removing any dead wood and any overgrown shoots.
Escallonia, Hypericum, Kerria, Philadelphus (established small- and medium-sized varieties) Cut out oldest one third of shoots after flowering.
Lavender Trim back dead flower heads after flowering and trim bushes fairly hard towards end of summer.
Rhododendron Carefully remove dead flower heads only.
Spiraea (small species) Cut out oldest one third of shoots in mid spring.
Wisteria Shorten all long, whippy shoots to six buds in mid summer and then to two buds in winter.

important to anchor the branches well; you can expect them to be ready for separating from the parent plant about two years after pegging down.

28 Shrubs: cutting back

Lightly cut back the dead flowering shoots on early summer-flowering shrubs as the blossom fades. Apply a top-dressing of proprietary rose fertilizer immediately afterwards.

29 Rhododendrons and azaleas: dead heading

Pull away dead flower heads from rhododendrons and azaleas.

30 Hedges: clipping

At the start of the season, cut hedges for the first time since autumn, clip them once again in the second half of the season.

31 Wisterias: pruning

Around mid season, prune wisterias by cutting back the long whippy shoots to about 25 cm (10 in), or six buds from the base.

Other Ornamentals

32 Feeding

Give liquid fertilizer every two weeks to all ornamentals, particularly to fast-growing plants that are approaching flowering time; they are using up nutrients very quickly at a time when they need them most.

33 Annuals and perennials: dead heading

Dead head all herbaceous annuals and perennials throughout the summer. This lessens the likelihood of diseases becoming established, as well as stimulating the production of new flower buds. The only exceptions are those plants from which you wish to save seeds for re-sowing next year. With small types of plants bearing massed flowers, such as bedding plants, the easiest way to dead head is with a pair of single-handed shears.

33 Continue to dead head herbaceous annuals and perennials throughout summer. Use scissor-like 'snips' on small plants with flower clusters to avoid cutting out too much.

34 Bedding plants: planting out

At the start of the season, as soon as the danger of frost has passed, remove half-hardy bedding plants from the cold frame, or other hardening-off area, and plant out in beds and containers. Immediately after transplanting, water them with a solution of liquid fertilizer.

35 Dahlia cuttings: planting out

At the start of the season, as soon as the danger of frost has passed, plant out young dahlia plants taken from cuttings in the spring or bought afresh. A cane stake generally gives adequate support in the first season and should be inserted before the plant.

36 Anemones: planting

Early in the season in mild areas, make a few further plantings of 'De Caen' and 'St Brigid' anemones, which will then flower in the late autumn.

37 Annuals: sowing and thinning out

Early in the season, complete the sowing of hardy annuals and, when the seedlings emerge, thin them out promptly to the spacings recommended.

38 Biennials: sowing

Early in the season, sow biennials for flowering next year. But only do so if you have room to spare in the vegetable plot or elsewhere – such plants as wallflowers and sweet Williams are large and slow growing and will occupy garden space unproductively for many months; if your garden is small, it is wiser to buy plants in the autumn. Sow them thinly in rows approximately 25 cm (10 in) apart. Thin out the seedlings to leave spaces of approximately 10 cm (4 in) between plants.

39 Watering

Water the ornamental beds in dry periods: most annuals are shallow rooted and suffer quickly in periods of dry weather. Plants in containers must be watered at least weekly; those in hanging baskets often need daily watering throughout the summer. Apply a liquid fertilizer once a week throughout the season.

40 Chrysanthemums: stopping

Chrysanthemum plants put outdoors towards the end of spring should now be stopped.

41 Herbaceous perennials: supports

Continue to give support to herbaceous perennials as they grow. With very tall-growing types, such as delphiniums, it is usually necessary to replace the canes with longer ones two or three times during the season. Using canes that are longer than the plants looks unsightly.

40 'Stop' chrysanthemums by pinching out the tip of the main stem. Side-shoots, which bear the flowers, then develop in the leaf axils. Gradually pinch these out, over a few days, until you have about eight left.

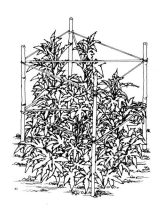

41 The appearance of tall, stately delphiniums can be spoilt if they are allowed to grow crooked. Use canes and string or wire supports to prevent this.

42   Sweet peas: care

From time to time, pinch out the side-shoots of sweet peas to encourage bushiness and more flowers. As soon as the flowers begin to mature, pick them regularly. Don't allow the sweet peas to set seed for, once this occurs, the plant's energies are directed away from the production of more flowers. Maintain the soil around the plants in a moist, but never waterlogged, condition and use a liquid fertilizer every two weeks.

43   Primulas: lifting and dividing

As soon as the flowers have faded on spring-flowering primulas, lift and divide the plants. If this is done every two or three years, the plants will have a much better chance of maintaining their vigour

44   Bulbs: cutting back foliage

Cut back the foliage of the later spring-flowering bulbs six weeks after their flowers have faded.

45   Tulips: care

As the flowers fade on hybrid (but not species) tulips they may be removed (carefully) from their growing positions to make way for annuals. Transplant the tulips to a plot in the vegetable garden or elsewhere until the foliage turns yellow and dies back. Then lift the plants and allow them to dry off away from full sun. Cut off the dead stems and leaves, then dust the bulbs with flowers of sulphur to prevent them from rotting. Store them in paper bags for re-planting in the autumn. Similarly, lift any daffodils, narcissi or other bulbs which have been growing in containers.

46   Irises: care

Cut back the foliage on pot-grown winter-flowering irises and place them in the hottest part of the garden – the rhizomes benefit from the heat.

47   Bearded irises: care

Around mid season, as the flowers fade on bearded irises, cut out the old flower spikes. Divide and re-plant the clumps every third year: discard the old, moribund growth in the centre . and use fresh, vigorous pieces of rhizome from the periphery. In a shallow planting position arrange the rhizomes with the upper part visible above the soil, ensuring that all fibrous roots are firmly anchored.

48   Rock-garden plants: care

Clip back the dead flower heads on spring-flowering alpines and other such plants and give them a light top-dressing of bone-meal.

49   Ponds: weeding

Pull out the blanket weed as it builds up in the pond; but do not use chemical algicides which leave a mass of dead, decomposing remains in the water. Use a stick, a wooden rake or, best of all, if the pond is small enough, lay a plank across so that you can reach in and pull out the weed by hand.

50   Beds: digging over

Towards the end of the season, dig over ornamental beds that are due to be re-planted in the autumn, removing perennial weeds and digging in well-rotted manure or compost.

43   1. Division is a simple way of increasing your plant stock. Every two years, when flowers are finished on spring-flowering primulas, use a fork to loosen the soil and ease out the clump.

2. Gently brush off as much of the soil as possible from the roots, being careful not to damage them, then pull the clump apart into four or six pieces. Cut out dead or damaged roots and re-plant the divisions immediately.

47   Every third year dig up bearded irises for division. Cut off strong single rhizomes from the periphery and discard the old centre. Fork compost and bone-meal into the soil and scoop away a shallow planting position for each fresh piece of rhizome, which should have roots and leaves of its own. Taking care not to bury them too deeply, plant them with the roots well-anchored and the upper parts exposed.

Fruit

51 | Weeding

Use a Dutch or similar hoe between the rows of soft fruit plants in dry weather. But take care not to hoe within 10 to 15 cm (4 to 6 in) of raspberry canes as this could damage the roots – and, in any case this area should have been covered with a weed-suppressing organic mulch earlier in the year (see SPRING TASKS **42**). Pull weeds or grass away from the bases of young fruit trees too; at the age of about six years, those growing in lawns can safely be grassed right up to the trunk.

52 | Soft fruit: watering

Don't neglect the soft fruit garden when watering. Most soft fruit are shallow rooted and suffer seriously from water shortage, which results in a small, tasteless crop. A sprinkler placed adjacent to the fruit cage will operate as effectively as one sited inside.

53 | Fruit cages: securing

As the crop ripens, make sure that the netting of fruit cages is secured against birds: check carefully for any holes and for gaps at ground level under which birds can enter. Repair immediately if necessary.

54 | Pests and diseases

Check soft fruit regularly for outbreaks of pests and diseases. Gooseberry sawfly larvae or magpie moth caterpillars on gooseberries and currants can strip foliage bare; they should be sprayed with derris. But never spray any plants with insecticide when the flowers are fully open and they are being visited by pollinating insects.

55 | Soft fruit: picking

Pick soft fruit as they ripen; a few days delay in a damp summer can result in the fruit succumbing to *Botrytis* disease. But don't be tempted to spray fungicide on to ripening fruits before picking.

56 | Raspberry canes: care

After raspberries have been picked, cut out the old canes from the base and re-tie in the new growths. As the canes grow during the season, tie them to the horizontal wires.

57 | Raspberry beetle

If, in previous seasons, your raspberries have contained the small larvae of the raspberry beetle, it is wise to take precautions. It is a difficult pest to control, and is almost always present when wild raspberry or blackberry plants grow nearby. The only effective remedy is to use a chemical spray: immediately after the flowers have faded, apply derris, which is not necessarily the most reliable control but I prefer it to the alternatives – malathion and fenitrothion.

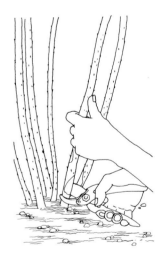

56 To make room for the new canes to develop, raspberry canes which have fruited should be cut back to just above ground level once the fruit has been picked.

52 The shallow roots of most soft fruit plants demand regular watering if you are to get the best quality fruit. A sprinkler positioned just outside the fruit cage will provide this.

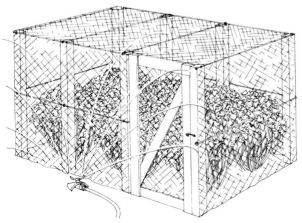

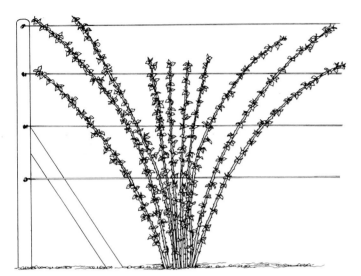

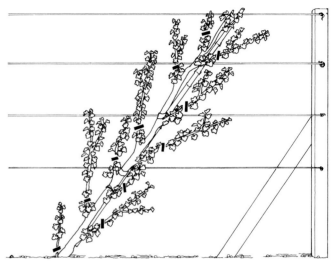

58 Tie last year's growth, which will be producing berries in the current summer, in to the outside of the fan pattern, thus leaving room in the centre for the new growth to develop. This also helps prevent any diseases in the old canes from passing to the new.

58 **Berries: tying in**

Tie in the new growths on blackberries and also on loganberries and other hybrid berries to keep them towards the centre of the fan pattern and away from the fruiting canes.

59 **Gooseberries and currants: pruning**

In mid season, summer prune cordon-trained gooseberries and red and white currants. Shorten all side-shoots to a point just above six leaves from the base and pull away any suckers or shoots growing at the base or from below soil level; do not prune the main shoot in summer. If you start summer pruning too early in the season, it merely encourages the proliferation of more side-shoots.

60 **Strawberries: care**

As strawberries begin to ripen, lay straw on the soil around the plants to prevent the fruit from touching the soil and rotting. But,

as with other types of fruit, do not spray with fungicide if any mould can be seen.

After the fruit has been picked from strawberry plants, use a pair of shears to cut back the foliage to about 10 to 15 cm (4 to 6 in) above the crowns. This stimulates new growth, which can then be encouraged further by applying a top-dressing of blood, fish and bone fertilizer at about 34 g per sq m (1 oz per sq yd). As runners appear, cut these off close to their origin or they will weaken the parent plant.

61 **Strawberries: virus**

If strawberry plants that are more than three years old have a poor crop, virus has probably built up in the stock. In this event, remove and destroy the plants and dig a fresh bed, incorporating as much well-rotted organic matter as possible. Order new, certified (virus-free) plants; they should be planted at the end of the summer, spaced with 45 cm (18 in) between plants and about 75 cm (30 in) between rows.

59 Prune cordon-trained gooseberries and red and white currants in mid season – not before. Cut back all side-shoots to just above six leaves from their bases. Suckers and shoots growing at the base should also be pulled out.

62 Prune new side-shoots on peaches and nectarines back to one leaf beyond the base cluster.

64 Forked stakes are one of the simplest means of providing support for old stone-fruit trees. Insert some form of padding, such as rubber or sacking, between the fork and the branch to prevent damage being caused through rubbing.

62 Peaches and nectarines: pruning

Prune wall-trained peaches and nectarines early in the season before the shoots become hard and woody. Complete the summer pruning as soon as the fruit have been picked.

63 Peaches and nectarines: thinning out fruit

Further thin out the fruit on peaches and nectarines to leave one approximately every 20 cm (8 in). Start when they are the size of hazelnuts. As the fruit begin to ripen, pull and, if necessary, peg back any surrounding leaves to expose them fully to the sun's warmth.

64 Stone fruit trees: supporting

The wood of plum trees is very brittle. To prevent branches from breaking under the weight of fruit, use stakes or other props to support them. Indeed, it is worth permanently supporting the branches of all old stone fruit trees because the likelihood of damage is so great. In years with a very good fruit set, thin out the fruit at the start of the season, leaving about 8 cm (3 in) between each fruit cluster; this not only lessens the likelihood of branch breakage but also ensures that individual fruits are larger.

65 Plums: pruning

Immediately after plums have been picked, prune free-standing trees by cutting out dead and damaged branches and thin out the crown slightly to prevent overcrowding. On fan-trained trees, cut out any dead shoots and shorten to three leaves those shoots that were stopped at six leaves during the spring. It is wise to prune established plants as little as possible – any pruning that is necessary must be done as soon as possible after fruiting because

later in the season freshly cut surfaces are prone to infection by the fungus which causes the very serious silver leaf disease.

66 Apples and pears: spraying

As petals drop on young trees of the later-flowering varieties of apples and pears, apply a final protective spray against scab before the fruit are picked; use benomyl, thiophanate-methyl or carbendazim. This is especially important if they are growing near to old trees, which are almost always affected with the disease.

67 Apples: codling moth

Almost inevitably, there will be some damage to apple fruit from the larvae of the codling moth. On large and old trees, nothing can be done to prevent this and some losses must be expected and accepted. On young trees, spray with derris as soon as the petals drop from the blossom; repeat about three weeks later.

68 'Fruitlets'

Collect up the numerous small apples – and, to a lesser extent, pears and plums – that fall from trees at the start of the summer. It is a perfectly normal happening – in Britain often called the 'June drop' – and is simply a means for the tree to rid itself of fruit in excess of those it has the nutrients and water resources to mature.

69 Cordon-trained apples: pruning

Towards the end of the season, summer prune cordon-trained apples to keep the trees under control and to let light and air in to the fruits. Cut back long side-shoots to a point just above three leaves from the base cluster, and cut back any smaller shoots arising from these side-shoots to a point above one leaf from the base.

65 Prune plum trees as soon as possible after the fruit has been picked. Exposed cuts later in the season will be vulnerable to the fungus which causes silver leaf disease. Established trees require little more than the removal of dead and damaged branches and a thinning out of the crown.

69 Prune cordon-trained apples by taking long side-shoots back to just above three leaves from their base cluster and sub-laterals to above one leaf from the base.

Vegetables

70 | Watering

Pay careful attention to watering the vegetable plot throughout the summer. If the amount of water available is limited, water crops when the parts that are to be eaten are maturing: for instance, cabbages as the heads are swelling, peas as the pods are filling, and potatoes as the tubers are swelling (this is roughly when the flowers appear).

71 | Tomatoes, peppers (capsicums) and aubergines (egg-plants): planting out

At the start of the season, as soon as the danger of frost has passed, tomatoes may be planted outside in soil or in growing bags. In milder areas, plant peppers (capsicums) and aubergines (eggplants) also. In cooler regions, the latter two, which are slower growing than tomatoes, will not have a long enough period in which to mature any fruit; however, in marginal districts it may be worth trying peppers under tall cloches. Space the plants with about 45 cm (18 in) between each. Pinch out the side-shoots of cordon tomato varieties grown up supports; do not do this with bush varieties.

72 | Runner beans: planting out

At the start of the season, as soon as the danger of frost has passed, plant out runner beans raised in the greenhouse and hardened off in the cold frame. If you have not already prepared a trench, dig in well-rotted manure or compost to the planting area and apply a dressing of blood, fish and bone fertilizer at about 100 g per sq m (3 oz per sq yd) as you do so. Place one plant on each side of bamboo canes arranged in a row with 15 cm (6 in) between each cane; alternatively, plant them in pairs, about 15 cm (6 in) apart around a 2 m (6 ft) high wigwam, either made of canes or of strings attached to a central cane.

72 | In a garden with space for a row of runner beans, place one plant on each side of a bamboo cane.

73 | Cucumbers and marrows: planting out

At the start of the season, as soon as the danger of frost has passed, plant out ridge cucumbers and marrows (or courgettes [zucchini]) raised in the greenhouse and hardened off in the cold frame; two plants of each vegetable provide an adequate crop for an average-sized family. Plant them in a bed prepared with well-rotted manure or compost dug in to a depth of about 30 cm (12 in). The plants may be allowed to sprawl over the soil surface although a small plastic sheet or other protective material such as straw should be placed beneath to prevent the fruit rotting. Alternatively, the plants can be trained up bamboo canes, the side-shoots being pinched out to keep the plants compact; cucumbers especially suit this treatment. In small gardens they can be grown in growing bags.

74 | Peas: sowing

At the start of the season, as you pick from the first sowings of peas, make further sowings of early or second early varieties at three-week intervals until mid season. Then sow a first early variety which will grow fast enough to give a crop in the autumn; use a dwarf type for this and place cloches over the plants as the weather turns cool.

75 | Carrots: sowing

At the start of the season, pull roots of the first sowings of early carrots; continue to pull the maincrop varieties from late-spring sowings throughout the summer. Sow further rows of maincrop varieties for autumn harvesting then, around mid season, switch back to a few quick-growing early types for swift results. From early to mid season also, sow the slower-growing so-called 'autumn' types for harvesting in early winter.

73 | 1. Spread some form of protective material, such as straw, beneath cucumber and marrow plants to prevent them rotting.

2. An alternative method, especially for a garden with less space, is to train the plants up canes, side-shooting them regularly.

76 Dwarf beans: sowing

Early in the season, pick from the first sowings of dwarf beans, then continue to pick and make further sowings at two-week intervals until mid season. Place cloches over the last-sown plants towards the end of the season.

77 Beetroot: sowing

Early in the season, pull roots from the first sowings of beetroot and then continue to sow at two- or three-week intervals until early in the second half of the season. Continue to pull roots as they swell. Beetroot are much tastier when pulled small – ideally they should be about golf-ball size.

78 Kohlrabi: sowing

Early in the season, pull plants from the first sowings of kohlrabi and continue to sow a few at two-week intervals until early in the second half of the season. After mid season, you will generally achieve better results from the hardier purple varieties for early winter harvesting. Always pull the plants when they are no larger than tennis balls; later they can become woody.

79 Lettuces: sowing

Continue cutting lettuces as they mature and make sequential sowings, putting in a fresh row of seeds as the seedlings from the previous sowing emerge (on average, this will be every ten days). Stop sowing summer lettuce varieties about one month before the end of the season and use cloches over the last two or three sowings in order to speed up maturity and obtain good plants well into the autumn.

Towards the end of the season, sow overwintering lettuce. Use the same technique as for the summer crop but choose a variety suitable for spring cutting. Better results will be obtained if the plants are covered with cloches. In order for lettuces to mature during the winter, you must sow a suitable variety in a cool greenhouse (see **21**).

82 Although new asparagus plants need two seasons before all the stems can be cut, once established they can remain in a permanent bed for many years to come.

80 Earth up potato plants about once a week until the leaves from adjacent rows of plants touch.

80 Potatoes: care

Continue earthing up potatoes until the leaves from two adjacent rows of plants are touching. Then water the plants regularly: the first new potato tubers should be ready for digging approximately 12 weeks after planting.

81 Radishes: sowing

Continue pulling from the early sowings of radishes and make further sowings at approximately weekly intervals; make sure that the plants are well watered in order to prevent them from becoming hard and tasteless. Stop sowing around mid season; after this the plants will almost certainly run to seed.

82 Asparagus: cutting

Continue cutting asparagus for about the first month of the season; after this the crowns will be weakened. Cut the stems about 6 cm (2½ in) below the ground. Once cutting has stopped, give the plants liquid fertilizer every two weeks.

83 Parsley: sowing

In the second half of the season, make a further sowing of parsley. Remove the plants from last summer's sowings when they start to run to seed and when the plants from this spring's sowings are large enough to use.

84 Spring onions (scallions): sowing

Continue pulling spring onions (scallions) and sowing fresh rows every two or three weeks throughout the summer.

Towards the end of the season, sow spring onions for harvesting in the spring. These are grown in the same manner as the normal spring onion crop but you must choose a variety designated as winter hardy.

85 Winter radish: sowing

Towards the end of the season, sow winter radish, using the same technique as with the summer crop (see SPRING TASKS **58**). Keep the newly sown seeds moist.

86 Tomatoes, peppers (capsicums) and aubergines (eggplants): harvesting

Towards the end of the season, harvest tomatoes, peppers (capsicums) and aubergines (eggplants). It is especially important to cut them regularly in order to stimulate young fruits on the plants to swell.

87 Cucumbers and courgettes (zucchini): harvesting

Towards the end of the season, harvest cucumbers and courgettes (zucchini). Cucumbers, especially, respond to being picked regularly; young fruits often abort when there are still several mature ones on the plant.

86 Harvest peppers (capsicums) and aubergines (eggplants) as soon as they are ready. This will encourage other young fruits to develop.

93

AUTUMN

As the shadows lengthen and leaves blaze with the fires of autumn, the gardener enjoys the last mellow days of golden sun while preparing for the colder weather to follow. Beds and borders glow with hot, rich colour, trees are heavy with fruit and the vegetable garden is filled to abundance with produce. Boston ivy (left) turns, within the space of a few days, from green to a stunning wall of scarlet.

AUTUMN NOTES

Autumn sees the last stages in the growth cycle of most plants before they retreat into winter dormancy. The seeds in the feathery heads of the grass *Pennisetum villosum* will be scattered by the wind. *Sedum* 'Autumn Joy' will gradually turn darker and darker red until cut down by the autumn frosts. Brilliant rose hips will be eaten by birds and so the seeds will be spread.

The end of the life cycle of a leaf is marked in many cases by a brilliant change in colour (*right*). Photosynthesis ceases and chlorophyll is no longer produced. Yellow pigments previously masked by the green chlorophyll now appear and in some species, particularly acers, new red, yellow or orange pigments are produced.

Stages of Growth

Gardeners develop a great affection for their plants, an affection that often takes the form of referring to seedlings as babies and of the process before pricking out as weaning. I have never heard slightly older plants called adolescents, although really ancient specimens are often accorded the privilege of a personal name. Interestingly, it is not very widely realized that plants do pass through stages of life, in much the same way as people and animals do.

During their early stages of growth many types of garden plants produce rather different foliage from the kind they have later. Species such as delphiniums that have dissected leaves when mature begin with leaves that are scarcely indented at all (sometimes, the change can be seen progressively down a single shoot). The leaves of the familiar Monstera, which is popular as a house plant, only develop their characteristic holes as the plant attains full size. Many palms pass through stages in which the leaves gradually 'fray' to produce the finger-like pattern typical of the mature plant. Ivy bears juvenile

indented leaves almost continuously but, from time to time, an upright shoot with more or less diamond-shaped mature leaves and bearing flowers appears. In most instances, these effects are of no practical aesthetic importance, but there are a few species that are pruned fairly hard each year specifically to induce a proliferation of young shoots; the classic examples are the many species of eucalyptus which have relatively boring adult foliage but young leaves that attract flower arrangers as moths to a lamp.

But in autumn we are reminded most of the later stages in life. Annuals die down and die out, the survival of their kind being left in the safety of their seeds. The autumn foliage colours, those most glorious manifestations of this time of the year, are merely the death throes of leaves that are no longer useful: the production of chlorophyll comes to an end as photosynthesis ceases – an irreversible process. Unlike young leaves which lose chlorophyll in the dark but produce it again when placed in the light, the old leaf is on a slippery slope from which there is no escape. The yellow appearance of autumn leaves comes from yellow pigments previously masked by the green chlorophyll, but the glorious red colours are brought about by the production of new coloured substances of different types (most notably, red- and blue-coloured anthocyanins or yellow- and orange-coloured xanthophylls).

When these processes of ageing occur in fruits, rather than leaves, it is called ripening. During this process, fruits produce minute quantities of a gas called ethylene which, in turn, hastens the ripening of other fruit nearby. Hence the basis in fact of the old trick of placing a banana among stored green tomatoes to ripen them – bananas are particularly efficient at ethylene production.

Seeds and Fruits

For biology and art teachers, seeds and fruits are some of the most reliable stand-bys. They also provide gardeners with a ready method of multiplying their stock, birds and other wildlife with a valuable source of food and, of course, plants with the means of survival. And, quite incidentally, many of them are beautiful. The production by plants of fruits and seeds is one of the most familiar sights of the autumn garden. But why are they so varied in size, shape and colour, how do they achieve their objectives and how may we make use of them?

I am not entirely sure that the distinction between a seed and a fruit is as widely known as it should be. A seed is the individual body that contains an embryo plant. The seed also contains a small supply of food, which enables the embryo to grow to a size where it can develop leaves and, thus, begin to manufacture its own nutrients. A fruit is a larger body within which seeds are borne and from which they derive protection; usually, they also have some structural feature – such as wings or prickles – that provides a means of being dispersed.

Among the common fruits that occur in autumn gardens, there is great variation in the numbers of seeds: they could range from the single seed of plums and damsons – I think some of the confusion between seeds and fruits has arisen because a few types of fruit contain only one seed – to the several thousands in a poppy head. Colours vary too: although many seeds are fairly uniformly brown, others are black, yellow, red, occasionally green or even blue. And there is a wide spread of size, from the tiny one-seeded plumes of clematis to the massive 'Bramley's Seedling' apples or prize-winning pumpkins.

But the greatest variation of all is in shape – for instance, the 'keys' of the ash tree, the acorns of the oaks and the numerous firm, fleshy 'berries' of pyracanthas and many other ornamental shrubs. I use the word 'berry' with caution because, like so many popular fruit names, it is often used incorrectly: almost all of the edible 'berry fruits' that we grow (strawberries, raspberries, loganberries and blackberries, for instance) are not berries at all whereas cucumbers and tomatoes are. In fact, strawberries are not even fruits, but the swollen tips of the flower stalk covered with masses of single-seeded fruits that we refer to as pips. Almost invariably, the variation in fruit shape is related to fruit dispersal. Large, round, plump fruits are those with a massive food store that attracts birds or mammals, those with plumes or other parachute-like contrivances are designed to be blown by the wind, and the numerous prickly or sticky types adhere to the coats of animals.

There is much to be said, when planning the autumn garden, for selecting some ornamental plants solely for the beauty of their fruit.

In many species of plant, the seeds are surrounded by a huge, plump foodstore that we call a fruit, designed to attract birds and animals. Over the years, gardeners have cultivated such species – apples (*right*), for example, or pumpkins (*above*) – with the aim of increasing size or improving flavour.

The silvery, silky seed heads of *Clematis orientalis* (*above*) are as attractive as the orange-yellow flowers. They are composed of a mass of ovoid seeds, each attached to a feathery tail which will carry it on the wind.

Perennial Growth Habits

The enormous diversity of plant life is one of the great joys of gardening. It is expressed in many ways: flower shape and colour are the most obvious. But plants vary in other ways too, most notably in growth habits – taking the form of shrubs, trees, bushes or climbers, for instance – which influence many autumn tasks.

Leaving aside annuals, which are over and done with in the course of a year, it is simplest to divide the remainder of garden plants – the perennials – into those that have a permanent woody framework and those that do not. The non-woody types are those, such as lupins, delphiniums, peonies and Michaelmas daisies, that make substantial summer growth which dies fairly soon after the onset of the autumn frosts. These dead shoots remain standing starkly above ground and, in most instances, are best cut down, shredded and consigned to the compost bin. I say 'in most instances' because there are some exceptions: any gardener with a care for bird life will want to leave at least a few seed heads through the winter – not only do these provide birds with valuable food, they also serve to distract them from the even more succulent buds of soft fruit bushes. And in most areas, there are a few garden perennials that are not absolutely hardy – hydrangeas and fuchsias are common examples – which derive some frost protection from having their dead, above-ground framework left until the spring.

But woody plants display a particularly wide range of form – from enormous trees to prostrate shrubs and many different types of climbers. Gardeners often find it difficult to decide how much to leave to its own devices, how much to train in a particular direction and how much to cut back each autumn. The best way to make a decision is to consider what are the gains and losses of the different courses of action? Persuading a plant to grow in a particular direction may be aesthetically pleasing (topiary is the extreme example), it may enable the plant to fill and use a space more effectively (a fruit tree trained against a length of wall, for instance), and it may encourage more productive cropping through inducing flower rather than leaf-bud formation.

There are few hard and fast rules. A pear tree allowed to grow to its maximum height in the open may be perfect for one garden, whereas training it as an espalier against a house wall may be more appropriate for another. I can, however, offer two guidelines that *are* generally applicable: first, removing the top part of a shoot encourages buds lower down to develop (or, as the old gardeners put it, 'growth follows the knife'); and, second, pruning should follow soon after flowering so that the old, spent flower heads are removed before the next crop of flower buds has formed. While there is certainly plenty of dead material adorning your plants in the autumn, therefore, think what you want it to do for you before cutting it all away in the cause of tidyness.

Climate and Weather

The Irish have a word for it, a word that conveys the condition better than anything I know. They call it 'soft': the wonderful all-embracing but very gentle rain that throws the colours of autumn into heightened contrast and brings out a lushness of green growth everywhere – the very green growth, of course, that is so characteristic of the Emerald Isle itself. Rain is Nature's water supply, just as the sun is the promoter of warmth, and as is evident to every gardener, plants need them both. But

The wide variety in growth habits of perennials is emphasized in a border planted in one colour. Dahlias, sedums and *Penstemon hartwegii* will all need to be dug up or cut back after the first aumtumn frosts. The shrub *Cotinus coggygria* 'Royal Purple' should be planted in a position, as at the back of this border, where it can grow without the need for pruning.

the overall features that influence plant life, not only in autumn but at all other times, are only partly met by rainfall and only partly by warmth. They are summed up by two more general and often confused words: climate and weather.

Weather is the sum total of the day-to-day conditions of rainfall or other forms of precipitation, temperature, wind and cloudiness, whereas the climate of a region is its prevailing long-term weather conditions. For plant life climate is much more important. There are many instances in gardening where the difference can be seen, but none more graphic than the colours of autumn foliage. The autumn tints of maples in North America are astonishing, not only because of the splendour of the colours but also because of the greater intensity of

The intensity of colour of autumn leaves (*above* and *left*) varies from year to year depending on the weather. In a 'good' year, a succession of warm days and very cold nights – conditions often found in North America and central Europe – will stimulate the production of leaf pigments.

them compared with those of the same species in Western Europe. There may seem to be relatively little difference in the weather between the two areas, but taken on a longer week-by-week basis the North American climate is more extreme. On average, the days are warmer and the nights colder. And it is these conditions that stimulate the greatest production of the coloured leaf pigments.

Climate and soil together dictate which plants will grow in any particular garden. Many interrelated factors are responsible for shaping the climate and, here, I can do little more than hint at their fascinating patterns. Some are perfectly obvious, others are much more obscure.

The most important factor is the latitude of the garden: its distance from the Equator and the Poles. Then there is the distance from the

Glistening frost covering shrubs and lawn is a feature of autumn mornings, but shrubs or climbers planted in positions where they catch the first rays of sun can be damaged because the frozen tissues thaw very rapidly.

nearest ocean or sea, the altitude of the garden above sea level, the proximity of hills or mountains and its aspect. I always think of the aspect – in other words, the direction the garden faces – as the fine climatic tuning, for even two gardens on opposite sides of the same street can have rather different growing conditions, simply because one faces north and the other south. Here, however, we have reached beyond climate to what gardeners call microclimate. Even within the garden, within a single flower bed, there will be differences in temperature, windiness and relative dryness. The overall climate and the weather are still the same but only after several years' experience with your garden will you discover the effects that these tiny nuances can have on particular types of plants.

103

The Origins of Soil

As you set about converting the desolation of the well trampled end-of-autumn vegetable plot into the dark, rich clods that the winter's rain and frost will break down for you, spare a moment to think about how it all began. Plant life could not exist without soil and the processes that form it are as wonderful as anything that the natural world has to offer. They are also lengthy, as anyone who has tried to convert sub-soil to top soil will have learned.

Almost all soil began life as solid rock but all rocks, once exposed at the earth's surface, are liable to be eroded or broken down into small pieces. Different types of rock are eroded at different rates: those like sandstone and chalk, which are produced by deposits of sediment from older rocks, erode much more readily than the ancient rocks such as granite from which the sediments originate. Many factors contribute to this erosion. Rain, for instance, trickling down into cracks, can freeze and then force apart quite massive boulders. The rain that beats upon the rock surface at least partially dissolves minerals contained within the stone. The wind, rivers and sea then all play their parts, not only in eroding but also in transporting the materials considerable distances from their parent rocks: this means, of course, that while the underlying geology may dictate the nature of the soil in your garden, it often does not, especially if the garden is in a river valley.

The mineral matter, once settled on the landscape, still doesn't constitute soil. Its chemistry may be changed by the slightly acidic action of rain (not only the notorious, artificially produced 'acid' rain; all rain is slightly acidic through containing dissolved carbon dioxide from the atmosphere). And material will also be changed by the first – usually simple – forms of plant life that establish themselves on the crude material. Gradually, as these plants die, their remains are added to the mineral material to form the first organic constituents of the soil; this, in its turn, enables more advanced types of plant life to grow, which also contributes to the soil's make-up. Once animal life establishes itself, the chemical changes are extended because the mixing and blending are accelerated by animals moving around: it is calculated that up to 100 tonnes (100 tons) of soil per hectare (2 ½ acres) are moved by earthworms in a single year.

Soil Types

Soil is the most under-appreciated substance in the whole of gardening, a wonderful yet immensely variable material that is a microcosm of the vast variability of life itself. Yet most gardeners do not know what it contains, how it functions, whence it comes and whence it goes. I have always found the processes of soil formation fascinating, but the variability of soil is also remarkable.

There are three main components in soil: living matter, non-living matter and matter once living but now dead. It is the relative proportions of each of these types of matter that give a soil its structural and textural character. In the very broadest terms, soils are grouped as sands, clays and loams and, try as we might, the proportions of their mineral components cannot be changed. You can add sand to a clay soil until the proverbial cows come home, but it will make precious little difference. A soil composed principally of clay is water retentive to the point of being readily waterlogged, slow to warm up in the spring and

Rich, dark soil, fertile enough to support a host of plants, is composed of a complex mixture of mineral and organic substances. The plants that grow in it will also influence its make-up. However, the intensive cropping that takes place in a garden will deplete even the best soil if the nutrients used up by the plants are not regularly replaced.

difficult to work. Conversely, a sandy soil is free-draining and loses both water and nutrients rapidly, is quick to warm up but also quick to cool. But whether sands, clays or loams, the addition of dead organic matter to soils improves their structure. Of course, almost all soils naturally contain some organic matter, and in the extreme case of peat soils this can comprise almost their entire bulk.

The plant life that thrives naturally in any particular area and the types of plant that thrive in our gardens are those that relish the physical conditions that the local soil offers. But there is one other

major difference between the various types of soil that, in its effect on plant life, can even override these structural and textural variations. This is a feature of the soil's chemistry: a measure of its relative acidity or alkalinity, called the pH. A soil with a low pH is acidic, a soil with a high pH is alkaline; the entire scale runs from 0 to 14 with the mid point – 7 – called neutral. Most garden plants thrive best in soils slightly on the acid side of neutral but some of the loveliest images of autumn, many of the trees and shrubs renowned for their foliage colours, are provided by plants that prefer acid conditions, including some of the finest maples, the smoke bush *Cotinus*, *Parrotia persica*, *Fothergilla* and *Liquidambar*.

The Mysterious Fungus

The warm damp earth of autumn spawns fungi. Perhaps because they can be deadly or benign, beautiful or ugly, they have a reputation for being mysterious and the more unusual ones are gathered by armies of obsessive collectors, who rise at dawn and search dark woods for little umbrellas, spheres and curious elongated shapes. In the garden, less exotic mushrooms and toadstools spring up overnight on lawns.

These relatively obvious forms are just a few of the types of fungi that impinge on gardening activities. Indeed, even the examples that we see on lawns and in the leaf litter are not the entire organisms, but simply the reproductive structures arising from a vast, microscopic network of threads in the soil. These threads are similar to the moulds that grow on old cheese, damp bread or almost any other moist organic substance (mould is, in fact, a type of fungus).

Fungi are unique in possessing this thread-like body structure and in reproducing by spores not seeds. Furthermore, they lack chlorophyll and hence are unable to manufacture their own food by photosynthesis. This combination of characteristics means that fungi are neither plants nor animals; indeed, they enjoy a classification all of their own. For gardeners, the inability of fungi to photosynthesise carries the most important implications: because they cannot obtain nutrients from the air they must obtain it from somewhere else and this need is satisfied by other organisms, either living or dead.

The countless fungi that live in the soil obtain their food supply from dead plant and animal remains, and in doing so, play a vital role in converting such detritus into humus. This is not only an invaluable soil conditioner but also a nutrient source for other plants that, in turn, thrive on the remains of their fallen relatives. In the compost heap and leaf-mould pile too, fungi – along with other micro-organisms – play an essential part in the important recycling process.

But not all fungi are so benign in their attitude to their fellow organisms. Many species are not content with dead remains but live parasitically on plants and animals, sometimes – as with the rusts and many of the mildews – developing complex and sophisticated feeding apparatus that ensures the plant victim remains alive while being drained of its life blood. Yet others, like the grey mould *Botrytis*, have adopted a cruder approach to parasitism: their attacks generally result in the death of the leaf or twig on which they feed, but they have the versatility then to be able to continue feeding on the dead remains. Yes, the placid autumn garden, with its fairy-tale toadstools, is a false Arcadia that conceals life and death struggles just out of our view.

Acers – brilliant with red and gold leaves in the autumn – grow best in an acid soil. Although they can be grown in neutral soil, they will never give of their best in strongly alkaline conditions.

Fungi can be to the good or bad of the garden. If you see large, bracket-shaped growths such as the spore-bearing body of this *Pleurotus ostreatus* emerging from the trunk or branches of a living tree, it is an indication that the timber within is already well rotted.

PLANNING THE AUTUMN GARDEN

Essential Shrubs

It may be unoriginal, but I think that shrubs – and I define them as 'any woody plant smaller than a tree' – are the most important features of the garden. I say this for several reasons. They have a permanent above-ground structure and, thus, can offer at least some interest all year round while not dominating a garden as trees can. Moreover, shrubs offer a greater variety of appealing features than almost any other plant: flowers, fruits, leaf colour (and colour change in autumn), leaf shape, evergreen or deciduous habits, colour and texture of bark, colour and shape of buds and, of course, the overall habit of the plant, which can range from that of a large upright bush to a ground-hugging prostrate carpet.

In the garden, shrubs can also be used in a variety of ways: as the permanent structural skeleton of a mixed border, as specimens in a lawn or other open area (and even in containers on a hard surface), or with other shrubs in a shrubbery or dedicated shrub border. Choosing shrubs is, in many ways, similar to choosing trees: how large they will grow, and how quickly; how dense the cover will be; and how their colours will blend with those of other plants nearby. There is a great deal

to be said for choosing at least some shrubs before you decide on any other plants for a new garden. You need not be as strictly confined to the spring and autumn planting seasons as I advise you to be with trees. Container-raised shrubs can be planted at any time of the year, except when the ground is frozen. And if you need to change the arrangements as your garden matures they can be moved much more readily than trees.

Shrubs with particular appeal for the autumn are most obviously those with distinctive autumn foliage colours, but do not disregard those that have attractive fruits and late-season blooms. Among good shrubs for foliage colour are the smoke bush (*Cotinus*), the dogwood (*Cornus florida*), flowering currants (*Ribes*), the low-growing ground-cover shrub *Stephanandra incisa* 'Crispa' and some of the viburnums, especially the guelder rose, *Viburnum opulus*. For fruits, many of the shrub roses are excellent, especially forms of *Rosa rugosa*, cotoneasters, and pyracanthas (birds seem to be less attracted to the yellow berried forms such as 'Soleil d'Or'). Late-flowering shrubs of especial merit include *Caryopteris clandonensis* and *Abelia × grandiflora*.

Given full sunlight the bright pink flowers of the deciduous lavatera (*left*) will bloom throughout summer and well into autumn.

The infinitely varied hues of cotoneaster, hydrangea, berberis and fuchsia (*above left*) combine in a distinctive autumn border.

Cotinus coggygria 'Flame' (*above*) more than lives up to its name with a rich blaze of autumn colour.

Selecting and Positioning Trees

There is scarcely a garden that cannot be enhanced by trees and it is in autumn that their presence is most appreciated as seasonal leaf colour takes over from the floral hues of summer. But in few aspects of gardening are so many mistakes made as in the selection and planting of trees. And these are mistakes that can have costly consequences when an over-sized tree must be removed at a later date and leaves a very conspicuous gap.

Always check and double-check the ultimate height that will be attained by any tree before you buy it. I say double-check because garden-centre labels have been known to mislead, and standard reference books on the subject do sometimes vary – largely because tree growth itself can vary on different soils and in different areas.

Having ascertained the tree's ultimate height, a safe rule to follow is to not plant it closer to a building than one-and-a-half times this distance. There are two reasons for this. Some trees, especially if planted in heavy clay soils, can cause serious damage to foundations. But even those that do not will almost certainly form a dense, light-obstructing canopy; this will, of course, be more serious if the tree is planted on the shady side of the house and if it is an evergreen species, which will cast shade even when natural light levels are low in winter. Always look carefully at

When the primary colours of summer annuals and perennials have disappeared, the autumn tones of tree foliage come into their own. Autumn reds contrast particularly well with the bright green leaves of *Robinia pseudoacacia* 'Frisia' (*far left*).

A selection of small trees in containers, including an ornamental cherry and *Acer japonicum*, with the spectacular large leaves of a gunnera, provides autumn interest on a terrace (*above left*).

The deep burgundy leaves of an acer (*above*) justify its special position, planted as a specimen in a border.

This crab apple (*above right*) has the dual benefits of spectacular foliage and fruits in autumn and delightful blossom in spring.

the impact that any tree is likely to have on the surrounding area – even if it will not shade a building it may cast a shadow over a large part of the garden, severely restricting your ability to grow vegetables, fruit or other sun-loving plants.

To achieve the most reliable establishment it is wise to plant trees in early spring or in autumn, although container-raised trees can be planted at other times of the year. If you are obtaining a relatively unusual species from a specialist nursery, however, this will almost certainly be supplied bare-rooted in the autumn and you should be certain that the planting position is prepared in readiness.

Among the trees most suitable for their autumn leaf colour, the acers are pre-eminent. Choice is very often limited by availability and cost rather than aesthetic considerations but among the best of those commonly offered are *Acer palmatum* 'Ozakazuki' and *A. rubrum*. *Amelanchier lamarkii* is a good tree for small gardens for its blossom and tolerance of clay and strong winds alone, and it has fine autumn colour. Some of the birches such as *Betula jaquemontii* colour well. Many thorns (*Crataegus* species), *Liquidamber*, *Parrotia persica*, some of the ornamental cherries and crab apples and several *Sorbus* varieties, such as 'Joseph Rock', are also worth choosing for their leaf colour.

Choosing Tree Fruit

Tree fruits are the only edible crop plants that will form a more or less permanent part of your garden. So it is important to plan carefully, in respect of varieties, of the position that the trees will occupy and of the way that they are to be trained. It is easiest to consider varieties first because, although it is unwise to be dogmatic about their choice, there are certain very useful and general guidelines. The best way to select a variety that you actually find tasty – and, more to the point, that grows well and produces a tasty crop when grown in your area – is to visit a local commercial fruit farm, especially a pick-your-own farm. There you will be able to taste a wide range of types. But if this is impracticable, talk sweetly to your neighbours and ask them which varieties crop well in their gardens and if you may

sample the produce from them.

Apart from taste and suitability for the growing area, the most important factor relating to choice of variety concerns its pollination characteristics. Apples and pears require a second tree of different variety (or, very occasionally, with some apples a third tree) before the blossom can be fertilized and fruit form. (Most other tree fruits are self-fertile and therefore not so restricting). Your nursery will advise which varieties are most suitable to pollinate those that you have chosen. The need to have more than one variety suggests that the most sensible answer is to choose two that are complementary in their uses – one for cooking and one dessert variety, for instance, or one early and one late dessert variety. Alternatively, you could choose a family tree: one in which two or

more compatible varieties are grafted on to the same rootstock. In this way you can enjoy up to four different varieties even if your garden is only large enough to accommodate a single tree.

Having selected a variety, you must choose the rootstock on to which the variety is grafted. The rootstock dictates the ultimate height of the tree. Although the greatest choice is available with apples, it is a significant factor with all other tree fruits too. In general, smaller gardens are better with trees on dwarfing rootstocks; however, the more dwarfing the rootstock, the better the soil conditions and climate must be. (In colder areas and with poorer soils, a tree on a dwarfing rootstock planted in a large tub of potting compost in a sheltered position may be the answer.) But rootstock choice

is also important in relation to the form of the tree: the restricted types of training such as cordons are always better with a dwarfing rootstock, otherwise the amount of pruning needed is never-ending. Cordons offer the ability to grow a few fruit in a very limited area; or, conversely, if space is not so limited, to grow a very large number of different varieties.

The siting of fruit trees is relatively easy – at least in theory. Generally, they should be planted in the sunniest and most sheltered position available, on soil that is not prone either to rapid drying or to waterlogging (although all soils can be improved with manure, compost or other organic matter). However special considerations apply to some fruit. Sweet cherries must be planted where netting or other protection can be provided against birds; training them, fan pattern, against a wall is sometimes the only way of doing this. Peaches, nectarines and apricots must be given a warm, sheltered position (against a wall is ideal) but really succeed well only in mild areas. Figs, too, are best trained against a wall in most districts, but they differ from other tree fruits in that they *must* be grown in poor soil, preferably with their roots confined laterally to an area of about 1 sq m (1⅕ sq yd) by concrete slabs sunk vertically to form a bottomless chamber in the soil.

Grapevines can be grown outdoors but, unless the area is very mild, they will not crop adequately; a good guideline is to discover if there are commercial vineyards not far from your home. For many gardeners, however, a vine must be grown in a cool greenhouse or conservatory. But it is best to plant its roots just outside in the open soil, then train the main shoot inwards through a hole in the side of the building close to ground level. The soil should be very well prepared with well-rotted manure or compost because grapevines have a prodigious appetite. Make sure there is a water supply nearby for their thirst is prodigious too; and be certain that the greenhouse or conservatory can be well ventilated in summer – otherwise moulds will be a problem on the ripening fruit.

Espaliers and fan-training (*opposite above* and *left*) allow you to grow an abundance of fruit in a relatively small area. Such restricted types of training are invariably better when a dwarfing rootstock is used.

The 'Conference' pear (*above left*) is one of the most reliable croppers and ripens to a dark, russet-tinged green.

Pick plums (*above*) as soon as they are ripe. They do not store well so you have a good reason for using them as soon as possible.

Autumn Vegetables

The autumn vegetable garden has three quite separate facets. First, it provides a continuation of some of the crops that you have been enjoying fresh during the summer (although sometimes the last sowings were of hardier varieties or those more atuned to the cooler conditions that begin to prevail). Second, it is the time to harvest the crops that originate from warmer climates and that, in temperate regions, do not have time to mature during the summer. And finally, late autumn is the time for harvesting those vegetables that are to be lifted, not for eating fresh but for storing during the winter; these are described on page 149.

Of those in the first group, you should allow space for beetroot and carrots: those sown in the first month of summer should mature in the first month of autumn. Runner beans, cucumbers and courgettes (zucchini) will continue to crop until the first frosts. In most areas sweet corn matures around the end of summer and the beginning of autumn. Greenhouse tomatoes will crop well into the autumn months, and are best kept cropping until frosts arrive and the greenhouse space is required for overwintering other plants.

The most important plants in the second group are outdoor tomatoes, peppers (capsicums) and aubergines (egg-plants). As with the greenhouse crop, outdoor tomatoes may be grown either in growing bags or in the open soil. Unless you are very restricted in space, however, and are obliged to grow the plants on path edges or on patios (when growing bags provide the only possibility of a crop), outdoor tomatoes are much better in the open soil, with the plant positions rotated year by year. And while all greenhouse tomatoes are staked or are cordon varieties, requiring careful tying in and side-shooting, lower-growing bush varieties are a much better bet for out-doors. Not only do they require none of this careful attention, but they can be

Cabbages are a crop which you can enjoy all year round if different varieties are sown (*above*). The type of winter cabbage now called a 'Savoy' (*above right*) is easily recognized by its dark green, crinkly leaves and is a particularly hardy variety.

A vegetable that actually begins to crop in the autumn is calabrese (*right*), which has the additional advantage of being a 'cut and come again' plant.

There should be no difficulty in growing aubergines (eggplants) outdoors in mild areas (*above*), especially when they are given the protection of cloches.

protected by cloches, which provide some insurance against uncertain weather. Yields will always be lower than from greenhouse plants – 2 kg (4½ lb) per plant is a good average – and you should allow space for at least a dozen plants, arranged equidistantly with 50 cm (20 in) between each. As with greenhouse plants, allow nine weeks from sowing the seed in individual pots indoors and planting out, which should be done after the danger of frost has passed and the plants have been hardened off.

In mild areas aubergines (eggplants) and peppers (capsicums) are plants to be tried outdoors, although, even there, they really require the protection of tall, barn-pattern cloches. Include them in the crop rotation with tomatoes – you should obtain five or six fruits from each per plant, but very often only one or two will swell on each plant at any one time. Only when the fruit are picked will others begin to develop. Aubergines are slow growing

and require about twice as long as tomatoes before they are ready for planting out; they must be sown in a greenhouse or other warm place in late winter for planting out after frosts have passed. Peppers require about one-and-a-half times as long as tomatoes so bear this in mind when planning your sowings.

The one brassica that is worth growing in a relatively small garden begins to crop in the autumn. This is the form of annual broccoli called calabrese. The plants are fairly large – up to 1.5 m (4½ ft) tall – but have the advantage of being a 'cut and come again' crop; as you pull the spears, more will form. Even from six plants, you will obtain a satisfying yield (you could plant a much larger number and freeze the produce, which stores very well in this way). You will require about 1 sq m (1⅕ sq yd) of ground to use as a seed bed for sowing in late spring. Transplant after about six weeks into prepared soil, allowing a spacing of 30 cm (12 in) each way.

115

AUTUMN TASKS

1 Lawns: mowing

As the temperatures drop and grass growth slows down, raise the blade setting on the lawn mower and continue to mow occasionally throughout the season and into the winter if the weather turns mild and the grass continues to grow.

2 Lawns: feeding

In the first half of the season, apply a specially formulated autumn and winter lawn fertilizer; it contains a lower proportion of nitrogen than the spring and summer blends. At this time of the year use of fertilizers containing a high proportion of nitrogen predisposes the grass to infection by fungal diseases. Avoid those autumn fertilizers that contain a worm-killing compound; on balance, worms are more valuable than harmful in a lawn.

3 Lawns: controlling moss

Apply lawn sand for moss control at the start of the season and then, once the moss is blackened, use either a spring-tine lawn rake or, preferably, a small electric scarifier to remove both the dead moss and the matted thatch of accumulated dead grass. The material can safely be composted although moss takes at least six months to break down effectively.

4 Lawns: sowing or turfing

In the early part of the season, seed or turf new lawns, using autumn lawn fertilizer as a base dressing and following the same guidelines as in spring (SEE SPRING TASKS **2**).

5 Ponds: maintenance

Remove leaves from ponds; scoop them from the surface before they become waterlogged and sink.

6 Weedkillers

After the early part of the season, stop using weedkillers in the garden; as the temperature falls, they become appreciably less effective.

3 A box on an electric scarifier fills up quickly with dead moss and grass, so raking up the loosened material by hand afterwards is just as effective.

5 Deciduous shrubs and trees, such as this wonderful autumn *Acer palmatum* 'Dissectum' (*below*), may look attractive – but decomposing leaves on the bottom of the pond will severely deplete oxygen for plants and fish, so remove them before they sink.

Greenhouse

7 Fumigation

If you use the greenhouse for overwintering non-hardy plants, remove tomato, cucumber and other crop plants early in the season and slightly before their productive season is over. Although you lose the latter part of the crop, it does enable you to clear the greenhouse completely, and then disinfect and fumigate it. Take the remains of the crop plants to the compost bin and scrub down the interior of the greenhouse with a proprietary garden disinfectant; then use an insecticide and fungicide fumigant smoke which will kill any persisting pests or fungal spores. If the greenhouse contains grapevines or other permanent plants, delay the fumigation until the plants are dormant after leaf fall. The ventilators and door must be closed before fumigating and you should observe carefully the manufacturer's recommendations regarding the period the greenhouse must remain closed and the length of time necessary to air it afterwards.

8 Shading

At the start of the season, use a dry cloth to wipe off shade paint from the outside of the glass. In very sunny weather you can still provide individual shading if necessary. Check that all panes of glass are tightly fitted; re-putty or otherwise correct any parts that are defective.

9 Insulation

Fit plastic insulation to the inside of the greenhouse. The most effective type is double-film bubble plastic sheet, which can be fitted with drawing pins to a wooden frame or with proprietary clips to aluminium structures. This cuts down heat loss (and heating bills) by up to 40 per cent without causing diminution of light quantity and quality that might be harmful.

10 Ventilation

Continue opening the ventilators during the early part of the season and also in mild spells throughout the autumn. For this reason, make sure that insulation sheeting is not fitted over ventilator openings.

11 Heating

At the start of the season, before they are required in earnest, check that greenhouse heaters are working efficiently. Electric heating – in the form of thermostatically controlled fan heaters – is easily the most efficient although the most costly to install; in some countries mains supplies must be laid by a qualified electrician. It is wise to have some sort of alarm system that warns of a sudden drop in temperature caused by an equipment fault, and a small paraffin burner available to use in such an emergency.

12 Watering

Gradually reduce watering for all plants kept in the greenhouse until, by the end of the season, they are being given very little water – not more than once every two weeks. Use no liquid, or other, fertilizer.

13 Bulbs: forcing

At the start of the season, plant prepared hyacinth and other bulbs for forcing indoors during the winter. Use a peat-based potting compost (unlike bulb fibre, this provides the nutrient which is important if the bulbs are to be planted in the garden next year) and plant them so that their tips are just showing. Cover the whole with a black plastic bag and place it where the temperature will remain as close as possible to 5°C (40°F). Check the bulbs regularly after about six weeks; when they have green shoots approximately 3 to 4 cm (1¼ to 1½ in) tall, bring the bowl back into the

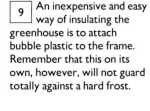

9 An inexpensive and easy way of insulating the greenhouse is to attach bubble plastic to the frame. Remember that this on its own, however, will not guard totally against a hard frost.

13 Plant larger bulbs like hyacinths with the tips above the compost level. Smaller bulbs like tulips should be completely covered. Black plastic will keep out light.

117

16 Several small buds develop on each chrysanthemum stem as well as the main bud. Pinch these out one at a time over several days to encourage the main bud to produce maximum growth.

17 Hard-coated sweet pea seeds need encourage-ment to germinate. Soak them overnight in water and then nick them opposite the 'eye' if they do not swell.

greenhouse or into a cool room in the house where you can be sure that a temperature of about 10°C (50°F) will be maintained. Remove the black bag and place the bowl in partial shade at first, moving it after about a week into a situation with brighter light.

14 Annuals: sowing

At the start of the season, sow seed of a few hardy annuals for potting on to provide colour in the greenhouse in the spring – any low-growing types are suitable, particularly candytuft, dwarf calendulas, cornflowers and limnanthes.

15 Carnations and pinks: hardening off

At the start of the season, move rooted cuttings of outdoor carnations and pinks into the cold frame for hardening off.

16 Chrysanthemums: care

Early in the season, bring potted late-flowering chrysanthemums into the greenhouse for flowering. Check regularly for signs of pests; spray with derris if aphids or caterpillars are seen. Disbud, by removing the side-shoots and leaving the main bud, for production of the best blooms.

17 Sweet peas: care

Just before mid season, sow sweet peas for flowering next year. Soak the seeds overnight before sowing, then make a small nick with the point of a knife in the seed coat opposite the 'eye' of any that have failed to swell. Sow the seeds in pairs approximately 1 cm (½ in) deep in 8.75 cm (3½ in) diameter pots of peat-based seedling compost. Once the seedlings have emerged and produced two true leaves, pinch out the shoot tips. Then transfer the pots to a cold frame for the winter, scattering a few slug pellets around them.

18 Herbaceous perennials: pricking on

Around mid season, prick on the young seedlings of herbaceous perennials into individual 8.75 cm (3½ in) diameter pots, then about two weeks later transfer them to the cold frame. Perennials raised from seed usually establish better if they are grown on in the pots until next spring or, in many cases, until next autumn before being planted in the garden.

19 House and greenhouse perennials: protecting

Two or three weeks before the first frosts are expected, move house and greenhouse perennials such as azaleas back under protection. This will be about the same time that you find it necessary to turn on the central heating in your home.

20 Half-hardy plants: care

Two or three weeks before the first frosts are expected, bring in stock plants of pelargoniums, fuchsias or other half-hardy types needed for taking cuttings. Remove any dead or yellowed leaves and spray the plants with a systemic fungicide (benomyl, thiophanate-methyl or carbendazim) to protect them against grey mould (*Botrytis*).

Overwintered stock plants of pelargoniums will continue to flower; these blooms should be removed from time to time in order that the plants are not weakened – they will last for a very long time in vases.

21 Dahlias: care

In the second half of the season bring dahlia tubers in from the garden. After dusting with flowers of sulphur as a protection against rotting, they should be stored half buried in boxes of dry peat or ashes under the greenhouse bench; alternatively, make large envelopes from entire newspapers, put one tuber in

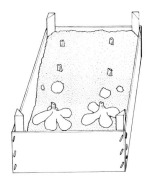

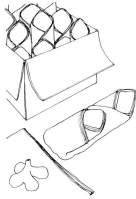

21 1. Store dahlia tubers in boxes of peat. Place them under the greenhouse bench to keep them cool.

2. Alternatively, make newspaper 'envelopes'.

each, leaving the top of the envelope partly open, and pack several envelopes together in cardboard boxes.

22 Chrysanthemums: lifting

In all except very mild areas, towards the end of the season, lift the stools of spray or other outdoor chrysanthemums from the garden and dust them with flowers of sulphur, then place in boxes of peat or ashes.

23 Primroses and primulas: potting

Towards the end of the season, dig a few primroses or hardy primulas from the garden and pot them into 8.75 cm (3½ in) diameter pots of peat-based compost in the greenhouse. They will then be forced into early bloom and can be used to bring colour both to the greenhouse and your home during the winter. The plants can be returned to the garden in the spring.

24 Lettuces: transplanting

Once tomatoes and other crops have been cleared from the greenhouse and it has been fumigated, transplant winter lettuces into the soil of greenhouse beds or into growing bags. Give soil beds a top-dressing of blood, fish and bone fertilizer and scatter a few slug pellets around the plants.

25 Checking

Towards the end of the season, re-check all plants that were brought in for overwintering, removing dead or yellowed leaves which can encourage grey mould or other diseases.

Keep a close check for any signs of aphid or other pest activity. If pests are found, promptly fumigate the greenhouse with an insecticide smoke. Read the manufacturer's directions carefully before use and temporarily move out any plants that are sensitive to the insecticide (see **7**).

23 Never underestimate the decorative potential of a greenhouse, particularly if it is as imaginatively designed as this one, with a complementing conservatory.

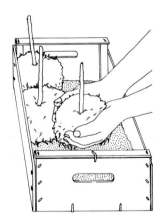

22 When chrysanthemums have finished flowering cut them off at about 15 cm (6 in) above ground and lift them out. Dust the stools with flowers of sulphur, then store them in boxes filled with peat or ashes.

119

Trees and Shrubs

27 Make sure young trees are securely staked before the onset of strong autumn winds.

28 1. Carefully trim off the stubs of broken branches with a fine-tooth saw.

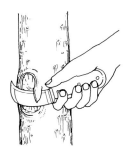

2. Finish off the trimming with a sharp knife and leave the wound to heal naturally.

26 Leaves

Rake up fallen leaves regularly, especially those close to drains and garden ponds, on paths where they can become slippery and hazardous, and also on lawns where they can quickly cause yellowing and damage to the turf. Unless they are very large and very numerous, leaves can be loosely forked into the surface of ornamental beds and borders, then top-dressed lightly with dried blood or sulphate of ammonia which aids their breakdown and enables them to form a protective mulch over the surface.

27 Young trees: staking

Check stakes on young trees: make sure that they are well secured and tied before the strong autumn and winter gales begin. Wind can not only damage trees directly but, by rocking them to and fro, it can cause a hollow to form in the soil around the base. This will fill with water which, if it freezes, could harm the stem tissues.

28 Branch stubs: trimming

Carefully trim off any broken branch stubs to enable wounds to heal and prevent decay-causing fungi from entering. Always use a fine-toothed saw and cut flush with – never into – the swollen collar at the base of the branch where it joins the main stem. Do not treat the cut surfaces with a proprietary sealing compound: for these have been shown to be potentially damaging.

29 Hedges: clipping

Before the middle of the season, clip hedges for the last time until spring. Don't wait until frosts are likely, when there is the risk of some shoot die-back and consequent damage from coral spot or other diseases.

30 Planting

Towards the end of the season, plant new trees and shrubs, especially those that are bought bare-rooted. Prepare a planting hole equal to about twice the volume of the root-ball. Fork in plenty of well-rotted manure or compost and a dressing of bone-meal at about 68 g per sq m (2 oz per sq yd), and spread the roots carefully. Hammer in a stout stake on the leeward side of young trees (so it is blown away from, not on to, the support) and secure it to this with a belt-pattern tree tie. Firm the soil in well.

31 Temporary plantings

Plants bought before their planting positions are ready should be heeled in temporarily by unwrapping them from the packaging and burying them about 5 cm (2 in) deeper than their normal planting depth. Plants that are properly packed will keep for about two weeks in a cool place if the top of the package is opened.

32 Deciduous trees and shrubs: cuttings

From mid season onwards, take hardwood cuttings of deciduous trees and shrubs. Half bury them in a slit trench in a sheltered part of the garden after laying a mixture of horticultural sand and bone-meal (about a handful of bone-meal to a gallon [4.5 litres] of sand) about 5 cm (2 in) deep in the trench base. The cuttings should root within 12 months.

33 Roses: pruning

Towards the end of the season, cut back very long growths on roses to prevent the plants from being rocked by strong winter winds. Ramblers can be more severely pruned: cut back the flowering shoots either to the base or to their junction with a main stem, depending on variety.

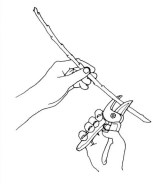

32 Choose a vigorous stem from the current year's wood and cut lengths of about 25 cm (10 in). The cut should be made just above a bud at the tip and just below a bud at the base. Plant them in a prepared narrow trench.

33 Check the variety of ramblers to decide whether to cut flowering shoots back to the base, as here, or the junction with the main stem.

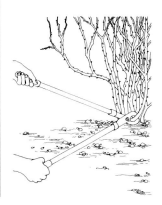

Other Ornamentals

 Herbaceous perennials: cutting back

As their flowers fade, cut back herbaceous perennials, although leave a few seed heads for the benefit of wild birds (this may also discourage them from the buds in your soft fruit garden). The dead stems should be chopped up and added to the compost bin.

35 **Herbaceous perennials: lifting**

From mid season onwards, the hardier herbaceous perennials, such as heleniums, Michaelmas daisies and geraniums, can be lifted, divided and moved. Leave until the spring the slightly more tender types and those more resentful of disturbance.

36 **Dahlias: lifting and storing**

As soon as the first frosts blacken their leaves, dahlias must be lifted. Cut down the tops to about 15 cm (6 in) above soil level, then use a fork to ease the mass of tubers from the ground. Poke out the soil from between the individual tubers with a small cane, then store them upside down indoors for about a week to dry slightly and allow excess moisture to drain away. Subsequently, they should be stored in a cool greenhouse or other frost-free place (see **21**).

37 **Soil: feeding**

As summer-flowering annuals are removed from beds and containers, fork in compost, scatter blood, fish and bone fertilizer at the rate of about 34 g per sq m (1 oz per sq yd), then

transplant wallflowers and sweet Williams seedlings for blooming next summer.

38 **Bulbs: planting**

From the early part of the season, plant spring-flowering bulbs of all types (except tulips, which should not be planted until the season's end). Be guided by the supplier's directions regarding planting depth for different bulbs, although, generally, most bulbous plants succeed well if the base of the bulb is at a depth equal roughly to two and a half times its average diameter. To lessen the chances of rotting, always plant bulbs on a layer of about 1 cm ($\frac{1}{2}$ in) of horticultural sand to which bone-meal has been added at the rate of approximately a handful per gallon (4.5 litres) of sand.

39 **Gladioli: lifting**

By mid season, lift gladioli, cut off the foliage just above the corms and allow them to dry for about a month in a frost-free place. Then store the corms in paper bags until the spring (see SPRING TASKS **36**). Any young cormlets adhering to the parent corms should be detached and bagged up for sowing separately in the greenhouse next spring.

40 **Chrysanthemums: lifting**

Before the soil freezes, towards the end of the season (in all except the mildest areas), cut back outdoor spray and other chrysanthemums to about 15 cm (6 in) and lift the stools. They can then be placed in compost-filled boxes and stored in the greenhouse over winter.

36 Once you have eased dahlia tubers out of the earth, remove any soil in the crevices with a blunt-ended cane, before storing them upside down for a week to dry slightly.

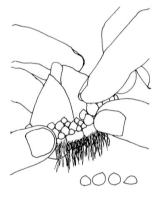

39 When gladioli corms have been lifted, remove young cormlets and store them in paper bags in a cool but frost-free environment. They can then be planted the following spring.

121

Fruit

$\boxed{41}$ How to choose a rootstock for common garden fruit trees

Apple
M. 27 Very dwarfing (will produce a tree 1.5 m [5 ft] tall) but only suitable for very good soils; very useful for vigorous varieties grown as cordons; trees will require staking permanently.
M.9 Dwarfing (will produce a tree 2 m [6.5 ft] tall); the best rootstock for general garden use; trees will require staking permanently.
M.26 Semi-dwarfing (will produce a tree 2.5 m [8 ft] tall); a very good rootstock for poorer soils.
MM.106 Semi-vigorous (will produce a tree 3-4 m [10-13 ft] tall); a better choice than M.26 for weaker-growing varieties.

Pear
Quince C Moderately dwarfing (produces a tree 3-5 m [10-16.5 ft] tall); the best rootstock for general garden use but not suitable for poor soils.
Quince A Moderately vigorous (produces a tree 4-5 m [13-16.5 ft] tall); the best rootstock for poorer soils.

Plum
St Julien A Semi-dwarfing (produces a tree 3 m [10 ft] tall although this restriction can only be achieved with careful pruning).
Pixy Dwarfing (produces a tree 2-3 m [6.5-10 ft] tall; this can only be achieved with careful pruning).

$\boxed{41}$ Ordering

At the start of the season, it is sensible to place orders for new fruit trees and bushes since demand for the more popular varieties may well exceed supply. Only buy plants which are raised by a reputable nursery and certified free from virus. When choosing tree fruits, especially apples, select varieties that are capable of pollinating each other. And you must choose not only a fruiting variety but also the rootstock on which it is grafted; the choice of rootstock is important for this will dictate the overall ultimate size of the tree.

$\boxed{42}$ Picking fruit

Pick apples, pears, plums and other tree fruits as they ripen. When fruit are ripe, they should part easily from the tree without being pulled. Apples and pears that are to be stored should be picked over carefully: reject any with blemishes, holes or bruises because they will rot rapidly; and never store windfalls or any fruit from which the stalk has been pulled. Apples should be stored in a cool, frost-free place (with a temperature as close as possible to 5°C [40°F]). They may be stored separately, not touching each other, and unwrapped on slatted shelves; alternatively, in batches of 10 or 12 in clean plastic bags partially closed at the top (the theory behind the latter method is that it limits the amount of moisture lost through the fruit). Pears should be picked when still under-ripe and checked frequently in store: because they are regularly disturbed, pears should be stored separately from apples, in a cool environment.

$\boxed{43}$ Cordon-trained apples: pruning

Complete the pruning of cordon-trained apples. Cut back any new side-shoot growth to a position just above one bud from the base. If, in previous years, there has been a great proliferation of such secondary shoots, (a fairly common happening in very wet areas), it is wise to delay all of the 'summer' pruning of cordons until the start of the autumn.

$\boxed{44}$ Winter moth

Early in the season, apply grease bands to the trunks of apple trees to trap the flightless larvae of the various species of winter moth as they crawl upwards to lay their eggs. Use specially formulated, not engine, grease; generally, it is more effective than greased paper bands, under which the insects can pass.

$\boxed{45}$ Trees: care

Early in the season, before the worst of the autumn and winter winds arrive, check the stakes and ties on all young fruit trees. Replace any defective stakes and loosen any ties that threaten to constrict the stems. Any jagged branch stubs on older trees should be cut cleanly to facilitate healing but only cut as close to the main trunk as the slightly swollen basal collar (*see* **28**) and do not use any proprietary sealing compound: the tree is likely to succeed better without.

$\boxed{46}$ Apples and pears: pruning

At the end of the season – provided the weather is not too mild and all the leaves have fallen – a start may be made on pruning free-standing apple and pear trees. Unless they have been neglected, old trees generally require very little pruning other than the taking out of dead or diseased wood and the removal of crossing or congested branches in the centre. But for young trees, formative shaping in the early years is very important. After pruning, do not treat the cut surfaces with a proprietary sealing compound: these are potentially damaging rather than beneficial.

$\boxed{44}$ Paint grease bands about 7.5 cm (3 in) wide around the apple tree, starting about 1 m (1 yd) above the ground.

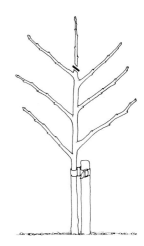

$\boxed{46}$ In the winter of its first year a maiden tree should have its main stem cut back to a height of 60 to 70 cm (24 to 28 in) above ground. Make the cut just above a bud.

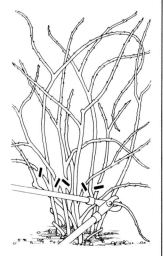

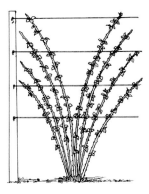

$\boxed{49}$ Remove about a third of the old wood on blackcurrant bushes. Cut back to a strong lateral shoot arising low down or right back to the base.

$\boxed{50}$ Cut back old soft-fruit canes which have fruited to just above ground level so that the new canes, which will fruit the following year, can be tied in to take their place on the outside.

$\boxed{47}$ **Strawberries: planting**

Continue with or complete the planting of new strawberry plants. If buying plants, choose the larger or 'jumbo' sizes, if they are available, rather than standard plants; they will establish themselves more rapidly.

$\boxed{48}$ **Weeding**

In dry weather continue to use a hoe to keep annual weeds controlled in the soft fruit garden, but remember not to hoe too closely to raspberry canes.

$\boxed{49}$ **Blackcurrants: pruning**

Prune blackcurrant bushes after the fruit have been picked. Aim to take out about one third of the old wood each year. Cut branches back to just above a strong side-shoot arising low down on the branch, or, if no convenient side-shoot exists, to the base. Because of the way the fruit are borne, blackcurrants benefit more from having old branches cut out than from having new growths shortened, unlike many other plants.

$\boxed{50}$ **Fruit canes: cutting back**

Once the fruit have been picked from blackberries, loganberries and similar cane fruits, cut back the old fruited canes to the base. Then re-tie the new canes outwards in a fan pattern to take the place of those that have just fruited (see SUMMER TASKS **58**); in this way, you make room in the centre for next year's new canes.

$\boxed{51}$ **Fruit cages: checking**

Check the netting on fruit cages and repair any holes: as soon as the weather turns cold and the natural supply of seeds becomes exhausted, bullfinches and other birds turn their attention to the buds on fruit bushes.

$\boxed{52}$ **Peaches and almonds: leaf curl disease**

As the leaves drop from peach and almond trees, apply the first of the twice-yearly sprays against peach leaf curl disease. Use Bordeaux mixture, or a similar copper-containing fungicide; make sure that the bark is sprayed very thoroughly since the causal fungus survives the winter in bark cracks and crevices.

$\boxed{53}$ **Wall-trained fruits: protecting**

If you live in an area with hard winters, towards the end of the season and before the worst of the frosts begin, erect protective screening over tender wall-trained fruits such as nectarines, figs, apricots and peaches (see SPRING TASKS **49**); in milder areas, it should only be necessary to protect the blossom in early spring. Use lightweight close-woven netting or plastic sheet secured to a light wooden frame; alternatively, secure a roll of netting to the wall above the plants and roll it downwards.

$\boxed{54}$ **Planting**

At the end of the season, plant new fruit trees, canes and bushes. For all trees, follow the planting method described for trees and shrubs (see **30**).

Bushes and individual cane fruits should be planted similarly, but with no support for bushes and with horizontal training wires for the canes. Check the recommended spacing distances with your supplier: because vigour varies considerably between different varieties, the inter-plant distances also vary. Blackcurrant bushes should always be planted about 2.5 cm (1 in) deeper than the soil mark indicated on the plant. Raspberry canes are most easily planted in a trench with about 45 cm (18 in) between plants and with 1.2 m (4 ft) between rows; the uppermost roots should be covered with no more than 10 cm (4 in) of soil.

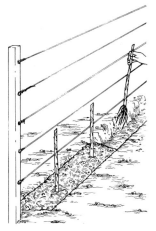

$\boxed{54}$ To plant raspberry canes, dig a trench about one spade deep. Fork into the bottom plenty of well-rotted manure or compost and a dressing of bone-meal at about 68 g per sq m (2 oz per sq yd). Plant the canes about 45 cm (18 in) apart in the trench, with the roots about 10 cm (4 in) deep.

123

Vegetables

| 56 | Carrot plants withstand frost fairly well and can be left in the ground over winter. Cut off the leaves close to the crown and protect them with a covering of straw.

| 58 | Once you have removed tomato plants, green fruit will continue to ripen indoors if it is kept in an adequately warm place.

| 55 | Weeding

Continue to use a Dutch or similar hoe in dry periods to keep annual weeds under control between the rows of vegetables.

| 56 | Protecting crops

Harvest crops as they mature. Beetroot and carrots may be lifted and stored in boxes in layers of sand, although in most areas they survive perfectly well in the ground. If leaving them in the ground, as a precaution cut off the tops without damaging the crown and lay straw around them, anchored with a scattering of soil; however, do not do this until the weather turns really cold at the end of the season because the roots may continue to grow beneath the straw to their detriment. So if necessary, wait until the start of winter before covering them.

| 57 | Cloches

At the start of the season, before frosts set in, place cloches over the later summer sowings of carrots, beetroot, dwarf beans, peas, winter radishes and other crops, as well as over parsley and Swiss chard plants that have been cropping through the summer.

| 58 | Tomatoes: harvesting

Early in the season, uproot the remains of the tomato crop. Take the debris to the compost bin. Take the green fruit indoors to ripen: any warm place is suitable for it is warmth not sunlight that brings about the ripening process.

| 59 | Cucumbers and courgettes (zucchini): harvesting

At the start of the season, before frosts set in, harvest the last of the courgettes (zucchini) and cucumbers and clear the remains to the compost bin.

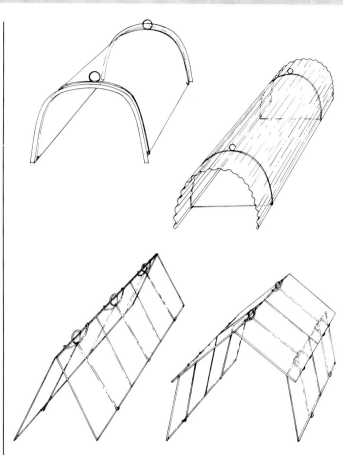

| 57 | Cloches have a wide variety of functions, from protecting plants to extending growing seasons. *Plastic sheeting (above)* over wire hoops is the cheapest form of cloche.

Robust plastic cloches (top and top right) with metal pegs are strong and simple to move around. *Glass cloches (above and above right)* with metal frames, although expensive, retain heat very well.

60 Soil: feeding

As crops are harvested, rough dig empty areas, forking in manure or compost as you do so: at this time of year, fresh manure may be used directly on the soil as it begins to rot down during the winter and thus does not cause any nitrogen depletion to growing plants as it does so.

61 Asparagus: cutting back

Early in the season, cut back asparagus foliage and mulch the plants with well-rotted manure or with compost.

62 Soil: pH tests

As the vegetable plot is cleared, take pH tests of the soil at several different points to determine if any lime is required: the ideal pH for vegetable growing is around 6.5. It is unlikely that lime needs to be added to any soil more than once every three or four years. If the pH has fallen, use the chart to estimate the amount of ground limestone you require to restore it to its ideal level; as will be evident, different soils require different amounts. Never add lime or fresh manure within one month of each other: the two substances can interact to liberate harmful ammonia.

63 Runner beans: clearing

After the first frosts, clear the remains of the runner bean plants and take them to the compost heap. (Dry the support canes, knock any adhering soil from within the hollow at the bases, then dip the bases in a proprietary garden disinfectant and store them for the winter.) Provided there have been no root rotting problems, it will be perfectly safe to prepare for next summer's runner bean crop on the same site: dig a trench about 40 cm (16 in) deep and work in plenty of manure or compost as you are re-filling it.

64 Lettuces: planting out

Transplant overwintering lettuces raised under protection for a spring crop, using well-ventilated cloches to protect the plants from the worst of the weather. Scatter slug pellets around the plants.

65 Broad beans: sowing

In mid season, sow seeds of hardy broad bean varieties for overwintering. In most years and in all except very cold areas, these generally produce the earliest crop in the spring although late-winter sowings very soon catch them up. Sow the seeds in beds with about 25 cm (10 in) each way between the plants.

---

62 Quantities of ground limestone in kilograms per square metre (pounds per square yard) to add to different types of soil to raise the pH to 6.5

Original pH (determined by soil test kit)	Soil type		
	Loamy sand	Loam	Clay
4.5	0.9 (1.6)	1.4 (2.6)	2.2 (4)
5.0	0.6 (1.1)	1.1 (2)	1.7 (3.1)
5.5	0.5 (0.9)	0.7 (1.3)	1.1 (2)
6.5	0.2 (0.4)	0.3 (0.5)	0.5 (0.9)

Using a soil-testing kit to measure pH

Small soil-testing kits can be bought from garden centres. Test the soil from several different sites in your garden. At each site decide on a testing area of about one square metre (one square yard) and take about five samples. Mix them together. Put a small amount of soil into the test tube provided with the kit and add indicator liquid according to the instructions. Allow the soil in the tube to settle and then compare the colour of the clear liquid with the colour of the chart to read the soil pH. A neutral soil is about 7: most plants, and particularly vegetables, prefer a soil that is slightly on the acid side (about 6.5).

WINTER

Winter has many guises, mild in some places, ferociously cold or snowy in others, but after the activity of the previous months the relative calm and austerity of this season provide the gardener with an opportunity to take stock, to plan and to appreciate the particular pleasures of a splash of colour in a bare landscape that would be lost in a summer border, or of a covering of frost on a few leaves.

WINTER NOTES

Hibernation

'What we need is a good hard winter to kill off these bugs,' gardeners are always grumbling. But what effect – if any – does very hard weather have on pest and disease incidence in the following year?

First, let's knock on the head the old adage about hard winters killing off the bugs and mild ones leading to outbreaks of pestilence. It's misleading to think in isolation of the (relatively few) creatures that can be regarded as garden pests. Nature is pretty even-handed in these matters and although the pests that die in very cold weather may survive in milder conditions, the same is true of beneficial animal life. So the predators, such as ladybirds, that naturally keep pests in check are also present in greater numbers after a mild winter. The position with the fungi that cause plant diseases is even more clear cut: no matter how cold the weather, the effect on tough, overwintering fungal spores is always fairly slight. Disease incidence in any season is much more closely connected to its intensity in the previous year (and thus the numbers of spores actually produced), and with the prevailing weather conditions in the spring – a wet early spring, leading to the successful germination of large numbers of spores, is of greater significance than a hard winter.

Generally, animal life is actually better equipped to cope with – and survive – freezing conditions than we are prepared to credit. After hard winters, it is almost invariably warm-blooded creatures – birds or the larger mammals (farm animals, especially) – that suffer. And they suffer because they must remain active throughout the winter period: long-term snow cover and frozen rivers and lakes deny them food and water. It is almost impossible for cold-blooded animals such as insects to remain active, because the functioning of their body chemistry is directly related to the prevailing temperature. When it is cold, they must slow down and those small, cold-blooded creatures, such as flies, that pass through the winter in an adult state invariably hibernate in well-insulated places.

Planning the Winter Garden

There is one school of garden design that suggests a garden should be planned to have appeal in the winter and that then the summer will automatically take care of itself. There is more than a grain of truth in this, and certainly if a garden is designed the other way around – for summer beauty – there is no guarantee that there will by anything to see for the cold months of the year. This is mainly because the plant kingdom can be subdivided into annuals, biennials and perennials.

The annual plant has a brief but often glorious existence, passing from seed through adolescence to maturity, flowering and producing its own seeds within the course of a single year. The annual illustrates perfectly the continuity of nature, the individual being merely an expendable medium for the continued survival of the species. And because the cold days of winter do not afford them good growing conditions, it is in seed form that annuals pass the winter months.

Biennials are fairly thin on the ground at the best of times. Only wallflowers and sweet Williams are really common in gardens; they are certainly evident in the winter garden as masses of foliage waiting to burst into bloom with the early warm days of the following season, although they, too, often find winter a hardship as their exposed leaves

Winter is the season when subtle colours come into their own, like the delicate greens and pinks of *Helleborus orientalis* and *Viburnum tinus*.

are battered by wind and cold and predisposed to attack by disease.

So the full burden of winter appeal in the garden falls upon the perennials. They all live for longer than one season although not, as is sometimes believed, forever. But not all of them are visible. The perennial takes many and various forms: bulbs, corms, tubers, swollen rhizomes and long fat taproots all protect the viability of the plant even though its above-ground parts may have died away.

What makes winter gardening so fascinating is the extraordinary variety of above-ground structures that *do* remain visible. The bare branch frameworks of deciduous trees and shrubs can appeal through their different traceries, through the colour and texture of their bark, the colour contrast between bark and buds and even, in a few instances, through the attractiveness of winter flowers. Indeed, it is in winter that I most appreciate the diversity of plant life. Summer spoils you, winter is the selective time, when only the hardiest can survive.

129

Snowdrops growing under a large tree (*above*) and hellebores in the shelter of a hedge (*right*) are both protected against the danger of rolling frost or frost pockets that can arise in a hillside garden.

The Importance of Topography

Topography is a matter of great – yet generally unappreciated – importance to gardeners. The topography, the surface configurations of the garden – whether it is flat or has slopes, humps and hollows – can determine if the winter is enlivened by particular types of blossom or if you must wait until spring before the blooms appear. It can even dictate whether particular types of plants will grow at all.

The more gardens that I see, the more I realize how very significant an element this is, and how much it varies from one site to another. It may take a fall of blown winter snow to reveal the irregularities in many gardens clearly, but on really sloping sites, of course, the effects are obvious. Cultivations may need to be confined to contour lines to prevent soil from being washed downhill, and terraces with retaining walls (well anchored and angled into the slope) are essential if the beds

and borders are to be anything more than temporary features. If you are fortunate enough to have land so varied that it includes a stream course or some other feature that results in slopes facing in opposite compass directions, a dramatic garden can be created.

It is in late winter and early spring that one very important topographical feature comes into its own. It is called a frost hollow and gains its distinctive character due to the fact that cold air is denser than warm. Where a garden, or part of one, is sited at the foot of a slope or is appreciably lower than the rest, cold air tends to roll downhill and collect in it. This means that the hollow is several, sometimes many, degrees colder at most times of the year. And when frosts are prevalent, they occur sooner and persist longer in the frost hollow than elsewhere. I have known instances where the existence of this feature only became apparent through particular plants repeatedly dying back as a result of frost damage to their young shoots; once they were removed to higher ground, they thrived perfectly well. In some instances, where the frost hollow is fairly shallow, repeated die-back and regeneration of the main shoots can result in bushy growth of the lower parts of a shrub or tree, which eventually grows normally once it manages to establish its leading shoot clear of the cold-air layer.

The Wild Winds

When a ferocious wind struck southern England in 1987, it destroyed 15 million trees in the space of four hours. Although this was an autumn wind rather than a winter one, and therefore a considerable proportion of the damage occurred because the trees were still in leaf and so presented a much greater surface area, as a demonstration of the sheer, physical force of the wind, the storm proved a point.

In gardens, it tends to be this type of damage (although usually on a less grand scale) that is associated with the wind. Branches fall from trees in most winters, fences are moved from the vertical and panes of glass are smashed in greenhouses and cold frames. In official statistics, a gale is a wind that exceeds about 35 knots and there are marked regional variations in their incidence. The areas that experience most gales are those where the wind first strikes land after having blown uninterrupted across a wide ocean.

However, it is not the regular gales that are the reason for the absence of trees from exposed regions. A soft, gentle breeze blowing almost constantly has more effect on plant life. Although it commonly carries moisture in large volumes (which it later deposits as rain), the wind is also a remarkably effective drying force — the reason we trouble to hang our washing outside. And the drying effect on plants can stunt their growth to a very considerable extent. The clearest demonstration of this is in cereal fields: if you bend down and look along the top of the crop, you will see how much taller the plants are, the closer they are to the shelter of the boundary hedge. The trees that *do* survive on exposed cliff tops and similar sites appear to be leaning permanently away from the prevailing wind direction — an illusion, because their misshapen form is due not to being blown but to the buds having been dried out and killed on the windward side.

The wind thus proves itself an adept pruning force, not just a crudely destructive one, and we should not forget the warm summer breezes on which insects and pollen are borne and many seeds dispersed.

131

Frost and Snow

Of course, the geographical location of the garden greatly influences the likelihood of there being any winter snow. Like rain, snow is a provider of moisture to the garden. But in contrast to rain, it is relatively inefficient: 25 cm (10 in) of snow contributes the same amount of moisture as only 2.5 cm (1 in) of rain. But snow falls at a time of year when most plant life is dormant and in need of very little water; however, it does have a rather more important role in the garden.

Snow is cold, of course, but can also keep what lies beneath it warm; this is the reason why Eskimos live in igloos. And in gardens, a covering of about 7.5 cm (3 in) of snow protects the underlying soil and plant life from being frozen. A good example of this is the contrast between the winters of 1947 and 1987 in Britain. During the first, much of the country experienced extremely heavy snowfalls and, although the cold weather persisted for a long time, there were few reports afterwards of valuable plants having been lost in great numbers. In 1987, however, most areas had little snow but prolonged intense cold; the soil was frozen for weeks on end and plant life suffered severely.

As well as forming an excellent blanket, snow is also very heavy. This is not a problem when it lies on the ground, but is potentially very

When heavy snow falls it can be a benefit to plants rather than a danger. The snow acts as an insulator keeping the plants beneath it warm and protecting them against severe cold. Snow should be knocked off branches (especially evergreens), however, in case its weight causes them to break off.

Illuminated by a wintery sun, a frosty winter garden (*above*) is at its most striking, but frost often destroys tender new shoots when it strikes late in the season.

Frost creates exquisite winter effects, enveloping a fine *Spirea arguta* (*above*) or a mass of wild clematis seed heads (*left*) in a cloud of silver.

133

harmful when it covers the branches of trees. Evergreens, with their large surface area, are most prone to broken branches: it makes sense to knock off the heaviest snowfalls as soon as possible.

The most familiar type of cold-weather damage is caused by the first frost of the year. The foliage of non-hardy plants blackens and shrivels as water is drawn from the cells, freezes and the resultant ice crystals puncture the delicate membranes. With hardy plants, the water seems to stay tightly bound within, but even they can suffer if an unexpected late frost catches their most tender young tissues (in the form of blossoms or young leaves). But in prolonged spells of freezing winter weather, with deeply frozen soil, roots as well as shoots are damaged. And, with evergreens, the low temperatures have an altogether different effect: because they bear leaves all winter long, the plants continue to lose water to the atmosphere (although conifers have developed elongated, waxy needles to minimize this), and more water must therefore be drawn from the soil to replace it. When the soil is frozen solid, this is impossible; hence, in a very long, cold winter, many evergreens die, not from the direct effects of cold but from drought.

Tracks in the Snow

In most areas, winter brings with it at least some snow. And although I have never been very excited at the prospect of launching myself down a ski slope, there are certain things about snow that I find especially appealing. In blanketing the garden, of course, it hides all my horticultural imperfections. But while it obscures so much, much is also revealed. One of my greatest winter pleasures, ever since childhood, has been venturing out into the garden when the snow is still undisturbed by human activity and following the non-human tracks and trails. This is how you can discover the wealth of creatures with whom you share the garden. Some are useful, some are not, but their presence underlines the value of the garden as a habitat for living things and not simply an appealing adjunct to your house.

Birds are attracted to the winter garden in large numbers; the more so if there is a collection of berrying shrubs, a bird table and, especially in very hard weather, a supply of drinking water (from an area of the pond kept free from ice by a small heater or from a continuously running fountain, for example). Birds' footprints are readily identifiable in the snow, and sometimes a series of tracks ends abruptly with a pair of wing feather imprints either side to mark a take-off point. Almost all birds should be considered friendly, although some bud-eating finches cannot resist unprotected soft fruit: the answer must be to protect the fruit, not frighten away the birds.

Small mammal tracks will be evident too. Rabbits, hares and squirrels venture across lawns and other open areas quite readily, but shrews and small rodents such as mice and voles are reluctant to stray far from hedgerows and other protection. Although such creatures do more harm than good to the garden, poison baits should be used only as a last resort. Trapping is an efficient means of control; but so is a cat, and it is often cat footprints that outnumber all others in the winter snow (and in these conditions of course, you have a unique opportunity of seeing where your pet goes in the hours of darkness).

You may be fortunate and see the footprints of some of the most important natural enemies of mice and voles. Weasels or stoats,

The winter garden is often a vital source of food for birds attracted by the brightly coloured berries of shrubs such as cotoneasters (*right*). Introducing a bird table and a supply of unfrozen water into the garden may make the difference between life and death for birds in a hard winter.

voracious little carnivores with extremely aggressive behaviour – and very sharp teeth – make tracks rather like those of kittens. No matter that these creatures are working on your side, you pick one up at your peril (unless wearing very strong gloves). Hedgehogs, moles and many other forms of animal life are there in the garden too.

In finding these tracks in the bare winter garden, who cannot fail to be fascinated. I have long believed that the gardener and the naturalist are but sub-species of the same being – one watching and studying wild things, the other trying to bend at least some of them to his or her will.

Hedges: Living Boundaries

Whatever the weather, inevitably there is a measure of restfulness and peace in winter after the frenzied gardening activity of the previous two seasons. I always welcome the break from the routine chores, for even in the mildest seasons, lawn mowing has all but ceased and hedge cutting is definitely finished. Strangely, however, I think about hedges more in winter than at any other time of the year. The main reason is because, once the annuals have gone, the herbaceous perennials have died down and most of the trees and shrubs have shed their leaves, the garden is bare and the hedges that form the boundaries, and sometimes divisions or windbreaks, are more dominant.

A hedge, whether created with carefully clipped evergreen yew (*above*) or less dense deciduous beech (*right*), provides important structural interest in a bare garden. A feature that is seen merely as a backdrop through most of the year takes on special prominence during the winter.

I am a great lover of hedges, of whatever species. Any living boundary is intrinsically more appealing and interesting than its wooden, brick or stonework counterpart. Of course, like anything else in gardening, hedges have their critics. They harbour pests, diseases and weeds, we are told. To some degree, this is true, especially in respect of perennial weeds, such as couch, ground elder and bindweed, which become almost ineradicable when spreading out from the safe haven of a hedge bottom. But the pest-and-disease argument is countered by the same reasoning that I used in relation to hard and mild winters: they harbour beneficial as well as pestilential creatures. Indeed, the balance with hedges falls even more firmly towards the beneficial since they provide important nesting sites for birds, which are among the most significant pest predators in our gardens.

A hedge is really a long, very narrow wood and, in consequence, is a microcosm of woodland life. You can spend many an interesting hour on your hands and knees peering into an old, mixed hedge at the different layers of plant life: the principal and secondary species, the herbaceous plants and climbers entangled in the centre, and the annuals at the base, which often flourish early in the season before the hedge itself comes into leaf and affords them too much shade. The holes and tracks made and used by small rodents will be visible too, as well as a multiplicity of insect life.

And many old hedges contain not simply a wealth of life but a wealth of history. Patient research has revealed that new species naturally colonize an existing hedge at a predictable rate. You can work out the age of a hedge quite easily. Assume that it has been allowed to continue unaltered and free from either significant artificial addition or removal of plants over the centuries, then by counting from one side along a 30 m (33 yd) run, the number of species of tree or shrub will indicate the age of the hedge in hundreds of years.

136

PLANNING THE WINTER GARDEN

Colour in the Garden

There is something to be said for designing the garden with winter in mind. If it looks good then, at least it will be tolerable for the remainder of the year. Certainly, in many temperate regions, the cold season is longer than the warm — barely four months are certain to be free from frost in many areas. The key to designing an attractive winter garden lies largely in choosing those few plants that flower then, have attractive foliage or bark and/or display an appealing shape.

Herbaceous perennials and annuals have almost all either died down or died out in winter. (Leaving the dead seed heads of some herbaceous perennials can give an interesting appearance to an otherwise dormant border, and, of course, birds will appreciate the bounty of the seeds.) But among herbaceous perennials the hellebores are notable exceptions in that their flowers are present throughout the winter, surrounded by the gradually dying leaves. The unfortunately named *Helleborus foetidus* is the most reliable.

Among trees and shrubs, a few — a rather choice few — can be guaranteed to flower at least during the milder spells. The winter-flowering cherry, *Prunus subhirtella* 'Autumnalis', has some of its pink blossom on display in all except the very coldest weather; the witch hazels (*Hamamelis* species) bedeck their bare branches with yellow or red stars; the yellow of winter jasmine (*Jasminum nudiflorum*) and the red of *Camellia sasanqua* brighten the dark days, winter sweet (*Chimonanthus praecox*) fills the air with the aroma of its small yellow blooms and *Viburnum bodnantense* also combines attractive flowers with perfume.

The dark red bark of *Cornus alba* 'Sibirica' (*below*) takes on a dramatic form in winter.

Colour comes from the bark and twigs of many of the dogwoods (*Cornus* species), several brambles such as *Rubus cockburnianus*, *R. phoenicolasius* and *R. thibetanus* and, of course, from the fruits of those plants that are left alone by the birds. The crab apple 'Golden Hornet' usually retains its golden fruits well and the white berries of snowberries (*Symphoricarpos*) are usually ignored by birds.

The choice of trees and shrubs with winter foliage colour is considerable. All evergreens clearly have something to offer, but it is worth paying especial attention to those with variegated foliage or with leaves attractively margined in gold or silver. A few evergreen shrubs — *Elaeagnus pungens* 'Maculata' is one of the best — have variegated leaves that really (rather than just apparently) intensify in hue in the cold months.

The success of winter-flowering bulbs is less dependent on the absence of frost than on their flowers not being damaged by rain. Several species of crocus flower fairly reliably in winter, the most notable being purple *Crocus laevigatus fontenayi*. Snowdrops, of course, flower in mid winter and are soon followed by the small red-purple of *Cyclamen coum* and by *Anemone blanda* (of which the blue forms are best). The earliest narcissi are usually the tiny hoop-petticoat daffodils (*Narcissus bulbocodium*), followed by the larger *N. cyclamineus* hybrids.

It is in winter that conifers and heathers really come into their own (*far left*), especially when their dark green tones are accentuated by a light dusting of frost. The burnished red of *Sedum* 'Autumn Joy' contrasts beautifully with deep winter greens.

The stark grey-silver bark of *Rubus cockburnianus* (*left*) is offset by the delicate flowers of *Helleborus foetidus*, one of the few herbaceous perennials to retain flowers right through the season.

The deep yellow flowers of *Jasminum nudiflorum* (*right*) cast a golden hue over the darkest of winter days.

Colour in the Greenhouse

Few things in the garden are as depressing as a disused and empty greenhouse. But there is no need for the greenhouse to be empty at all, or for its winter use to be confined to the function of overwintering tender plants from the garden or raising out-of-season vegetables. Any greenhouse can become an oasis of colour during the winter with the careful choice of plants.

If the greenhouse is unheated, re-name it an alpine house and use it to protect alpine and rock garden plants from the rain and clinging damp. I have described the setting up of an alpine house on page 33; among the numerous types of alpine plant are a few that are especially satisfactory for winter colour. Many of the primulas are excellent for this purpose: the fragrant *Primula marginata* and its hybrids, for instance, with show auriculas, their leaves covered with mealy dust, and *P. edgeworthii*, which has a dusty farina easily damaged by the outside rain. The tussocky species of *Androsace*, many tiny cyclamen and crocus species and, of course, the early-flowering saxifrages such as *Saxifraga grisebachii* and *S × kellereri* will all make you wonder why you never grew them before.

A greenhouse heated to about 7°C (45°F), in order to give frost protection to pelargoniums, fuchsias and other half-hardy perennials, offers you even greater – but different – scope. Here you can grow a wide range of half-hardy foliage plants, including those like coleus, with its bronze-red leaves, that are readily raised from seed. Among the begonias, too, are many with interesting foliage, such as *Begonia masoniana* (iron cross begonia), which derives its name from the purple cross on its bright green leaves, and the popular *Begonia rex*. You will also find that many flowering species bloom right through the winter months. The pelargoniums are easy to grow and will flower almost constantly provided they are given occasional liquid feeding. Pot plants such as hoya, the wax plant, several types of begonia, with their delicate shades of red, pink, yellow and white, and numerous others will delight and surprise you with their unexpected colours.

A winter greenhouse can create a spectacular effect in a bare landscape if used to house such flowering plants as these exotic orchids (*left*) or narcissis and stately arums (*below*).

Winter Containers

There is no reason to put away all your tubs and other containers once the half-hardy bedding plants of summer have been laid low by the first frosts. There are several ways of planting the containers for winter appeal, although you shouldn't be too ambitious: it is unrealistic to expect to have as many containers through the winter as you have in the summer. But the impact of even a few during this dark period of the year is welcome.

But, first, be certain that any containers to be used during the winter are frost-proof. You need to replenish the compost before re-planting; in smaller containers, discard all the old compost (it makes a useful organic addition to your garden soil) and replace it with fresh. In larger tubs, remove the top 10 cm (4 in), fork the lower layers to break up any compacted material, then add fresh peat-based compost and mix this in with the existing. It's important to take particular care when watering winter containers; not only do plants take up less water in winter but the lower temperatures mean that there is less evaporation and so composts can become more readily waterlogged.

If you want *reliable* winter flowers in your containers, the choice is very limited. Easily the most dependable choice lies with universal pansies. These have improved immeasurably in recent years and can either be bought as plants in the autumn or raised from seed sown in trays in early summer. Unfortunately, few seed companies offer single colours so if you require several plants of any particular shade, you need to raise rather a large number to be certain of obtaining your choice. Some of the coloured primulas also flower throughout the winter, although they are less reliable.

The bulbs that I referred to for winter colour in the garden generally (see page 139) can also be used in containers, as can small plants of almost any evergreen shrubs – in the spring, they may be removed for planting in the open garden. Even tiny conifers or other evergreen trees may be used successfully, and evergreen climbers – any of the numerous variegated ivies, for example – can be used to supply the trailing component that is especially attractive with winter hanging baskets. However, you should bear in mind that winter winds can be cold and many evergreens, including such tough customers as the ivies, tend to brown rapidly if placed in an exposed spot.

The fragile simplicity of snowdrops is beautifully emphasized by this stark stone urn (*below left*).

Container plants such as this viburnum (*below*) can of course be moved around to provide interest wherever it is needed most.

Statuary and Topiary

Ornaments are virtually eclipsed in summer by the extravagant colours of annuals (*below*). In the paleness of winter, however, the texture and colour of the stone are seen in their full beauty (*left*).

It is a mistake to think that plants are or should be the only structural features of the garden. Tubs and pots are important features and so are items that contain no plants at all but are purely ornamental in their own right. I have in mind statuary in its various forms, the presence of which is most apparent during the winter. Even in a relatively large garden, one carefully selected statue, placed at a focal point, can be immeasurably more dramatic than dozens of smaller ones. Indeed, it is remarkable how effective a statue can be at drawing the eye in a particular direction. If you have a prominently placed garden pond, you could place a figure in the water, or use the statue as an integral part of a pond fountain. The choice of ornaments is a highly personal matter and I would not presume to dictate what you should and should not have – although I record my fervent wish that you will not opt for brightly coloured gnomes. Nonetheless, I do caution restraint and patience when choosing statuary. After all, no matter how hard you try, it is almost impossible to like a statue that doesn't appeal to you immediately; love at first sight is the only maxim to follow, which is why I urge you to be patient enough to wait until you find the right item.

When seeking a statue, you will find there is considerable choice not only in pattern but also in quality and in materials used. Genuine old stone or lead statues are almost prohibitively expensive, but modern reproductions are now so good that they make perfectly acceptable alternatives. An attractive weathered appearance can be encouraged by painting the surface either with milk or with dilute cow manure, which stimulates the growth of algae, lichens and moss.

Of course, you can also have living statuary in your garden, statuary in the form of topiary. The clipping of shrubs into geometric or fanciful shapes is a very ancient art and one that requires patience.

Topiary training requires patience, but the result can be extremely attractive.

The best shrubs to use are necessarily small-leaved – yew and small-leaved box are ideal in cool temperate climates – although some good large specimens also exist in holly. However, they are all fairly slow-growing. The training should begin early. Sometimes the desired shape can be achieved simply with clipping. Or it may be necessary to tie branches in the desired direction initially. Especially with the more extravagant examples a permanent and durable iron framework is necessary. You can train topiary into any shape you choose but I must offer two pieces of advice: first, make absolutely sure that your topiary specimen is in the correct place – unlike a statue, you can't move it; and be warned against attempting two or more matching and identical pieces – there are few horticultural objectives that are more frustrating.

Statuary (*above*) is a very individual expression of taste and a wonderful opportunity for the gardener to make a highly personal mark on the garden.

Paths and Steps

Winter

Spring

Summer

A path is an important structural feature as well as having a major impact on the overall appearance of the garden through the way that it subdivides it into distinctive sections. If its construction is well thought out it can also be a feature of some attractiveness in its own right. Think carefully before laying out any path, especially one that is not the most direct means of going from A to B: you need a sound design justification for taking people on a longer route than they would naturally follow. This detour could be to see beds and borders that otherwise would be hidden. If the path curves out of immediate sight, so much the better for then it plays on natural curiosity, wanting to see what lies beyond.

If you have recently moved to the property there is much to be said for waiting a season before you lay paths of any substance. By then, the sunny, shady and otherwise blessed areas of the garden will have revealed themselves as suitable for plant beds or borders. Around these, routes will suggest themselves as you move about the garden. By the time the first year is ended, well-trodden courses will have appeared as if by magic. These can then be rendered more permanent. It is at this stage that monetary rather than design considerations begin to take over. Many paving materials are very expensive and it is important to spread your resources thoughtfully.

Years ago, I was faced with many, many metres of paving to lay, and I settled on two materials for the bulk of the walkways. For areas relatively close to the house that carry a good deal of traffic, I used gravel, confined within treated lengths of softwood, anchored in place with pegs. The base on which the gravel is laid ideally should be of hardcore,

This Italianate garden has specific charms in every season, from winter (top left), through early spring (far left), to the fullness of the summer months (left).

Steps, paved areas and paths (far right) offer excellent opportunities for imaginative touches in your garden.

although very well-rammed soil will suffice, especially if the soil is naturally clayey. In more rural parts of the garden, around and through trees and shrubs, I used similar wooden edging but the path itself was of chipped bark. Unlike gravel, this is not a permanent surface and needs topping up annually; but it looks ideal in such situations.

Only for very well-used routes do I use hard paving – stone or reconstituted stone or bricks – chosen as appropriate to match the material from which the house is built. I would strongly advise against wood for paths, despite the fact that it is often recommended. All wood becomes slippery and dangerous when wet and is a classic instance of garden designers choosing something for appearance rather than practicality.

Steps are essential in a garden that already has changes of level. But they are desirable even on a flat site where much extra interest can be achieved by deliberately introducing a sunken (or raised) area to which the steps provide access. Although it is possible to create steps of gravel by confining it behind wooden risers, this is rarely satisfactory and for reasons both of safety and appearance, it is important to have steps that are strongly built of properly bedded stone or brick.

The more extensive paved area, to which the name patio seems to have become inextricably attached, can also be of gravel but this is only really satisfactory if it is very large – what in my terminology is a courtyard. And even then, you will need a separate – firmer – brick or stone area on which to be able to place garden chairs and table. Plan very carefully before laying a patio. It must be close enough to the house for drinks, meals and other necessities to be carried easily. It must be in a spot that receives the sun at the time of day you require it and yet be capable of being shaded in some way (a pergola for more or less permanent shade, a parasol over a table for something simpler). And it must be large enough – there is nothing more frustrating than a patio so small that chairs tip backwards over the edge.

Marking the Boundaries

Almost every garden has its boundaries defined in some way. The structure used for the boundary must serve several quite different purposes, many of which become especially apparent in winter. First, it must mark the physical boundary so that there is no legal dispute over the matter: this is relatively simple and can be achieved merely with posts and single strands of wire. More importantly, the boundary should offer at least a measure of privacy without shading the garden unduly; it should offer shelter from the wind, both for the owners of the garden and for their plants, and, from a purely practical standpoint, it should be durable without being prohibitively costly. There are three main options: a fence, a hedge or a wall. For most gardens, a 2 m (6½ ft) high boundary will be adequate, lessening the strength of the wind for a distance of 20 times this height – 40 m (130 ft).

Fences are the cheapest type of boundary and the quickest to erect. But they are also the most prone to damage. It is important to choose a type of fence that has some permeability to the wind – one providing a 50 per cent barrier – in other words, with an equal number of gaps and wooden battens – will lessen the strength of the wind while minimizing the amount of structural damage. A 2 m (6½ ft) high fence should have supporting posts sunk at least 60 cm (24 in), and preferably 90 cm (36 in), into the ground. I would advise not fixing these posts in concrete but ramming the soil around them and then attaching diagonal posts to brace each upright. A 30 cm (12 in) high trellis attached to the top of a fence will enable you to train roses or other climbing plants along the top.

Walls are relatively quick to erect and, if properly bedded and buttressed, are robust enough to withstand wind damage but are also expensive and can look stark and dominating. They, too, can be softened by growing climbing plants over them, but it is important to choose a constructional material in keeping with the surroundings – old brick with old brick houses, stone with stone buildings and modern concrete blocks only with modern houses. The biggest practical drawback to a wall in a windy situation is not that it will be blown down, but that it will cause the wind to eddy on the leeward side with the result that large quantities of leaves or other debris will accumulate.

Once established, hedges are in most ways the ideal boundaries. They are permeable, flexible and therefore resistant to damage, attractive and provide shelter for wildlife (the shelter they also afford for pests, diseases and weeds can conveniently be overlooked). They are fairly expensive, but their biggest disadvantage is the time taken to mature. The fastest growing conifer hedges are not to everyone's taste; in any case, a fast-growing hedge will continue to grow quickly, so requiring regular trimming, and, in many situations, will soon become out of hand. Perhaps the ideal answer for a gardener requiring a quick boundary is to use a fence as temporary protection, but plant a hedge alongside, then remove the fence when the hedge is high enough.

The evergreen *Phlomis fruticosa* softens a brick wall (*below*).

The copper leaves of a beech hedge (*right*) create a secluded walkway.

Preparing Compost for the New Season

I cannot conceive of a garden running effectively without compost. A compost bin provides you with a supply of this invaluable organic matter, and at the same time offers a facility for the convenient disposal of most garden debris. A bin can, of course, be erected at any time of year, but the winter is particularly convenient because plant growth has ceased and most routine tasks are ended for the season. Moreover, there is a great advantage in having the bin prepared in advance of spring and the deluge of green matter this provides.

I have used the expression 'compost bin', and I do so advisedly because I am quite convinced that no other method of making compost is remotely as effective. Such a bin should be constructed of a cube of approximately 1.25 m (4 ft), with slatted sides but with no base and no top. The slats should be of treated timber planks, about 2.5 cm by 10 cm (1 in by 4 in) with gaps of about 2.5 cm (1 in) between each, secured by galvanized nails.

Ideally, the bin should be exposed to at least some rainfall as moisture is essential for the composting process. My compost bins are partly beneath a large deciduous tree and this provides an ideal degree of exposure, although during the height of summer it is sometimes necessary to run the hose-pipe on to the compost.

Almost all organic matter can be composted, although it is wise to exclude chicken carcasses and other animal waste from the kitchen as these can attract vermin. Woody matter is excellent provided it is first passed through a garden shredder. Leaves tend to block up the free flow of air and water through a compost heap as they decompose fairly slowly and are best stacked separately in a leaf-mould cage built of four posts and chicken wire. After every 15 to 20 cm (6 to 8 in) of debris have been added to the compost bin, scatter a proprietary compost accelerator over the surface or add a layer of fresh farmyard manure to provide a source of nitrogen for the decomposition bacteria. Compost should be ready for use within six to nine months.

A compost bin can be sited fairly close to the house if you screen it with trees or shrubs, but still leave it open to some rainfall (*above*).

Winter is a time for tidying up in the garden (*left*) before the pressure of essential daily tasks takes over again in spring.

Winter Vegetables

Spring

Apples (*above*) are among the very few fruits that can be stored for some time after picking.

Winter

Summer

Autumn

Varieties and growing methods may vary enormously with the seasons, but at all times of the year, from spring (*opposite right*), through summer and autumn (*far left* and *left*), some form of vegetable can be grown, even through to such crops as winter radish and perennial spinach in winter (*opposite left*).

In order to have fresh (as opposed to frozen) vegetables during the winter, you need to choose varieties carefully. A few crops can actually remain outside and continue to grow during mild spells, although in most areas they really do need the protection of cloches. Others will survive in the ground in a more or less dormant state, especially if given a little protection, and, of course, others can be raised in a cold greenhouse.

Among the winter vegetables to grow outdoors are winter radish. All varieties have larger roots than the summer varieties and some are very large indeed; perhaps the closest to the summer salad radish types is 'China Rose'. Sow it in exactly the same way as other radishes, but in mid to late summer, after the sowing of the others is over. Winter spinach is another vegetable that can be grown and picked in the same way as its normal summer counterpart. Sow it first at the end of summer and again in mid autumn, using either the variety 'Sigmaleaf' (which can be grown as a summer variety too) or one of the prickly seeded types such as 'Broad Leaved Prickly'. Sea kale beet or Swiss chard offer other forms

of winter spinach, but must be protected with cloches in most areas. Although most books advise giving parsley the protection of cloches too, it is surprisingly hardy and grows unprotected in many areas through most winters.

The hardy autumn carrot varieties such as 'Autumn King' are ideal for winter use. They may be lifted in mid autumn, their tops removed and the roots stored in boxes between layers of dry sand; but in most areas they will keep perfectly well in the ground. Wait until early winter when the leaves begin to die down, then cut off the foliage and cover the plants with straw, anchoring it with spadesful of soil; if this is done too early, before the start of winter, the roots will continue to grow under the straw cover, which will impair their quality. Parsnips may be treated similarly and are generally hardier than carrots, surviving in many regions even without a straw cover. Beetroot are best lifted: as their roots are rather more exposed at the surface, they are readily damaged by frost. But always twist off the leaves rather than cut them, to prevent 'bleeding' (the exuding of red sap).

Lettuce is the ideal winter vegetable

crop to grow in a frost-free greenhouse. Sow the seed in trays in early autumn, then transplant the seedlings into the soil bed of the greenhouse or into growing bags; the plants will mature in the second half of winter. I have found the variety 'Kwiek' best for this type of cropping.

Fruit are not as hardy as vegetables, and only apples and pears can be stored fresh. Even among them, the only types that can be left on the tree through the winter are a few of the very late apple varieties, including 'Sturmer Pippin' and 'Granny Smith' and the very hard pears such as 'Winter Nelis'. Apart from these few exceptions, apples and pears should be picked for storage, although it is only the later maturing varieties that keep satisfactorily – a factor to bear in mind when you are choosing new trees. Pears and apples should be stored separately because pears require checking regularly: they do not ripen very uniformly and should be eaten as soon as they are ready. I find that both apples and pears store best when laid unwrapped on slatted shelves or in slatted boxes, with adjacent fruit not touching each other. Place them in a cool but frost-free place.

149

WINTER TASKS

1 Never break the ice on a pond as the shock waves could easily kill fish. If you do not have a pond heater, melt the ice in one corner by pouring hot water over it. Make sure you choose a spot where there are no plants rooted underneath.

1 Ponds and fountains: maintenance

Take care not to allow ice to build up on the garden pond. If you have a fountain, much the best system is to leave it running throughout the winter: almost all modern pumps are designed to continue operating at low temperatures but do check the manufacturer's specifications first.

If the fountain is unsuitable or you prefer to turn it off, a small pond heater connected to the electricity supply will keep a small area free from ice. If you have no electricity supply to the pond, the simplest method of removing ice is to pour a kettle of hot water into one corner (but not where there are plants rooted beneath). Never smash the ice for the shock waves can easily kill fish.

Greenhouse

 Ventilation

During any mild spells open ventilators in the daytime, but always close them at night.

 Heating

Make sure that any heated greenhouse contains an accurate maximum/minimum thermometer; the thermostatic controls on electric heaters are relatively imprecise.

4 Checking plants

Regularly check plants brought in for overwintering and remove dead or yellowed leaves and dead flowers. If there are any signs of *Botrytis* grey mould, spray immediately with benomyl, thiophanate-methyl or carbendazim fungicides.

Keep a close check on all over-wintering plants for any signs of aphid or other pest activity. If pests are found, promptly fumigate the greenhouse with an insecticide smoke. Read the manufacturer's directions carefully before use and temporarily move into your house any plants that are indicated as sensitive to the insecticide: do not leave them outside in the cold.

5 Watering

Give very little water to plants until near to the end of the season, but do not allow their compost to dry completely. About two weeks before the end of the season, begin to give a little more water to start fuchsias, pelargoniums and other stock plants into growth. If they have been stored under the staging, lift them into full light and mist gently.

 Dahlias: care

Check overwintering dahlia tubers for signs of decay. If any are affected, remove them

immediately and give the remainder of the tubers a dusting with flowers of sulphur.

7 Crocuses: potting

Around mid season or when their leaves first appear above the soil, lift a few crocus corms from the garden. Pot them in 7.5 cm (3 in) diameter pots and bring them into the greenhouse warmth. As soon as the flower buds begin to colour, they may be taken indoors to brighten the home.

8 Cuttings: care

At the end of the season, provided the plants have started into growth, cuttings may be taken from fuchsias, pelargoniums and other stock plants. Dip the cuttings in a hormone rooting powder and strike them in the usual manner in a peat-and-sand medium in propagator trays (see SUMMER TASKS **18**), or directly into 8.75 cm (3½ in) diameter pots with some form of cover to retain moisture.

9 Cuttings: potting on

At the end of the season, cuttings taken at the end of last summer and kept in propagator trays should be potted on into individual 8.75 cm (3½ in) diameter pots of peat-based potting compost. Feed them with liquid fertilizer every two weeks.

10 Aubergines (egg-plants) and peppers (capsicums): sowing

Towards the end of the season, make the first sowings of those half-hardy vegetables that require the longest growing season: aubergines (eggplants) and peppers (capsicums). Both of them resent root disturbance, so sow them directly in 8.75 cm (3½ in) diameter pots ready for planting out later into growing bags or ring culture or other large

 Botrytis, or grey mould, is a very common, and serious, fungus disease, affecting fruit and plants in wet conditions. Combat it by spraying with fungicide.

 Crocuses provide wonderful winter colour in the home. Lift a few corms from the garden for potting in the greenhouse and bring them indoors when the flower buds begin to colour.

 Sow aubergine (eggplant) and pepper (capsicum) seeds directly into 8.75 cm (3½ in) diameter pots. Sow two seeds in each pot and remove the weaker if both emerge.

pots. Sow two seeds in each pot in a peat-based universal compost; alternatively, use a seed-sowing compost and apply liquid fertilizer once a week. If both seedlings emerge, pull out the weaker. Remember that greenhouse space is valuable so only raise as many plants as you really need: four or five of each should be adequate for the average family's needs.

⟨11⟩ Annuals: sowing

Towards the end of the season, sow those annuals that require a long growing season: among half-hardy plants, the most important are pelargoniums. These require a temperature of at least 21°C (70°F) in order to germinate, but thereafter the seedlings may be grown on in lower temperatures: an average of about 10°C (50 °F) ensures plants large enough to flower by the middle of summer. Among slow-growing hardy plants, antirrhinums (snapdragons) are the most important and should also be sown now.

⟨12⟩ Chrysanthemums: care

Check chrysanthemum stools for mould. Dust with flowers of sulphur if there is any damage or with derris if aphids or other pests are present.

⟨13⟩ Chrysanthemums: cuttings

Towards the end of the season, take cuttings from potted greenhouse chrysanthemums.

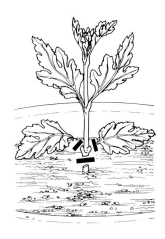

⟨13⟩ To propagate green-house chrysanthemums, cut shoots about 7.5 cm (3 in) in length, with no flower buds present. Remove the lowest leaves and strike the shoots.

Choose shoots close to the soil that are approximately 3 mm (1/10 in) thick and about 7.5 cm (3 in) long but with no flower buds present. Strip off the lowest leaves, dip the shoots in hormone rooting powder and strike them in a peat-and-sand medium in a covered propagator in the usual manner (see SUMMER TASKS **18**). There is usually space and time to take the cuttings now, but they can be left until the start of spring when outdoor chrysanthemums are also propagated.

⟨14⟩ Herbaceous perennials: root cuttings

Take root cuttings of phlox, romneya, Japanese anemone and anchusa. Cut pencil-thick pieces of fresh, vigorous root approximately 6 cm (2½ in) long, straight across the top and slanting at the bottom. You can then recognize the 'top' and 'bottom' of the cuttings and should plant them in the direction in which they were growing. Press them vertically into peat-based seed and cutting compost in 12.5 cm (5 in) diameter pots under a covered propagator.

⟨15⟩ Containers: preparing for spring

Take any opportunity to wash and clean pots, trays and propagators ready for seed sowing at the end of the season and in spring. First wash off any adhering soil or compost, then soak the vessels in a solution of a proprietary garden disinfectant, and finally rinse them in clean water.

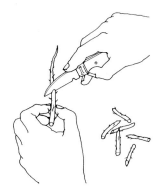

⟨14⟩ 1. Cut pieces of root approximately 6 cm (2½ in) long. It is important to plant a root cutting in the direction in which it was growing. So that you can recognize this, make a straight cut across the top, where it was cut from the parent plant, and a slanting cut at what was the lower end of the root.

2. Plant the cuttings vertically, with the straight cut uppermost. About 2.5 cm (1 in) of cutting should show just above the compost level.

Trees and Shrubs

procedures and precautions as for fruit trees (see **29**).

18 | Shrubs and climbers: pruning

At the end of the season, prune the hardier late summer-, autumn- and winter-flowering shrubs and climbers. Most require only a cutting back of the old dead flowered shoots; however, *Buddleia davidii* should be cut back much harder, all shoots being pruned to within about 30 cm (12 in) of ground level, and cut to a point immediately above a leaf cluster. Wisterias can be pruned earlier (around mid season) by cutting back to two buds from the base those shoots that were pruned to about six buds during the summer (see SUMMER TASKS **31**).

19 | Coral spot disease

At the end of the season, look out for coral spot disease on dead and moribund twigs. The symptoms are small salmon-pink pustules: any twigs bearing these should be cut out and destroyed because the fungus causing the disease can spread from dead to living tissues and bring about shoot die-back. Immediately after cutting out affected tissues, spray the surrounding healthy wood with thiophanate-methyl fungicide.

20 | Snow

After heavy snow-falls, knock off the snow lying on the branches of conifers and other evergreens: their large surface area can hold a great weight of snow which may cause the branches to snap.

---

17 Wear goggles when applying tar-oil spray. No other protective clothing is necessary but wash your hands or any part of the body which comes into contact with the spray.

19 Many trees and shrubs are susceptible to coral spot disease. Look out for the symptoms on dead and moribund twigs and take action before the disease can spread to living tissues.

16 | Young trees and shrubs: protecting

During spells of mild weather continue to plant trees and shrubs (see AUTUMN TASKS **30**); provide protection for all except the hardiest newly planted evergreens. A screen of hessian or woven plastic cloth could be erected on the side facing the prevailing wind, at least.

17 | Deciduous trees: care

Around mid season, providing the temperature is not below freezing, apply a tar-oil spray to any deciduous (not evergreen) tree that suffered seriously from pest attack during last year – especially if the infestation was by sap-sucking pests such as aphids or scale insects. Use the same

18 | Common late-flowering shrubs that require routine pruning:

Buddleia davidii Cut all shoots to within about 30 cm (12 in) of the base in late winter.
Ceanothus (deciduous) Cut back hard to a point three buds from the base of the flowered shoots.
Clematis (species) Cut back hard after flowering or in late winter to strong new buds about 20 cm (8 in) from the base or from the base of the previous season's growth, depending on the amount of pruning needed to keep the plant within bounds.
Hydrangea Cut out the dead flower heads with three leaves attached in early spring.

Other Ornamentals

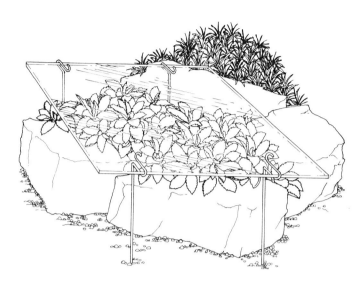

| 22 | Place a cloche or a sheet of glass over rock garden plants which are particularly sensitive to winter damp to protect them from rain. Support the sheet of glass on supports which you can make from sturdy wire.

| 21 | **Protection**

At the start of the season, before the worst of the frosts begin, place a protective mulch of peat, shredded bark or compost around the crowns of any plants that are only marginally hardy in your area.

| 22 | **Rock garden plants: care**

Check alpine and other rock garden plants regularly, and pull away any dead leaves that collect around them – these encourage rotting. In their natural environment many alpine plants are insulated by a crisp blanket of snow so they do not tolerate winter damp well. Protect softer or woolly leaved types against damage by rain and wet soil by placing over them an open-ended cloche or a single sheet of glass, which can be supported on sturdy wire supports.

| 23 | **Tulips: planting**

At the start of the season, complete the planting of tulip bulbs, placing a layer of sand in the planting hole to minimize the chances of rotting (see SPRING TASKS **36**).

| 24 | **Sweet peas: care**

At the start of the season, check sweet peas in cold frames and pinch out the tops.

| 25 | **Hardy seeds: sowing**

Sow the seeds of alpines and of trees, shrubs and other hardy plants that have a hard, tough seed coat in pans of sand; place them outdoors. The winter's frosts encourage the breaking of their in-built dormancy and they will germinate more reliably when brought into the warmth in spring.

| 22 | Alpine plants are particularly intolerant of damp. Pick fallen leaves off the plants to discourage rotting.

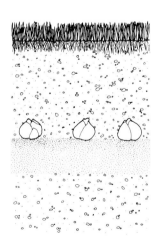

| 23 | Even if the soil in which you plant tulip bulbs is well-drained, a layer of sand in the bottom of the planting hole will reduce the risk of the bulbs rotting.

Fruit

| 26 | 1. When planting new trees dig a hole about twice the volume of the root-ball, forking in well-rotted manure or compost and a bone-meal dressing.

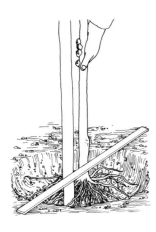

2. Insert a stake on the leeward side, then position the tree. The old soil mark on the stem should be level with the surface — use a piece of wood to check this.

3. Firm in the soil well and fit a belt-pattern tie.

| 26 | **Planting**

Continue to plant new fruit trees, canes and bushes (see AUTUMN TASKS **54**) but not during very cold weather and when the soil is frozen. If trees and bushes are delivered from nurseries during such times, store them in a cool place with the packing intact but opened at the top.

| 27 | **Apples and pears: pruning**

At any time during the season, carry out routine pruning of free-standing apple and pear trees (see AUTUMN TASKS **46**). With trees under about four years old, the formation of a well-shaped crown is the most important task. Do not treat the pruning cuts with a proprietary sealing compound.

| 28 | **Apples and pears: storing fruit**

Check stored apples and pears regularly. Remove pears as they ripen and also remove any fruit showing signs of decay.

| 29 | **Tar-oil winter wash**

Around mid season, apply a tar-oil winter wash to fruit trees, bushes and canes. This kills over-wintering eggs and adults of aphids and other pests and also eradicates algal and lichen growth on old trees. Use a powerful sprayer, dilute the concentrate exactly as the manufacturer recommends, and use a pair of goggles when spraying (inevitably a proportion of the spray will be directed upwards) (see **17**). With trees growing in lawns, some chemical will almost certainly fall on to the grass, which will turn brown temporarily then recover.

| 30 | **Feeding**

At the end of the season, apply fertilizer to all fruit plants. A top-dressing of sulphate of potash at about 17 g per sq m (½ oz per sq yd) is ideal, followed by a thick mulch of well-rotted manure or compost; alternatively, use about 68 g per sq m (2 oz per sq yd) of a general fertilizer such as blood, fish and bone unless the plants are already very vigorous and producing a great deal of leafy growth. Old productive trees generally require little feeding.

| 31 | **Raspberries: pruning**

At the end of the season, prune autumn-fruiting raspberries – those varieties that bear a fairly small crop of fruit towards the tips of the canes during their current season of growth – cut all the canes down to ground level.

| 32 | **Peaches, nectarines and plums: protecting blossom**

In mild areas, at the very end of the season protect the blossom on early-flowering wall-trained peaches, nectarines and plums by erecting lightweight close-woven netting or plastic sheet in front of them, although in cooler regions this can generally be left until the very early spring (see SPRING TASKS **47**).

| 33 | **Blackcurrants: big bud**

Towards the end of the season, look for signs of big bud (blackcurrant gall mite) on blackcurrants: some of the buds will be swollen to two or three times their usual size. If only a few buds are affected, cut them off and burn them, then, on a mild day, spray the bushes with benomyl (although this is primarily a fungicide, it also has some effect on mites including the species causing the big bud symptoms). If the bushes are extensively affected, however, it is likely that they are contaminated with the virus causing reversion disease which the mite transmits: the cropping and vigour will gradually decline and the plants should be replaced with new, certified stock.

| 33 | When the buds on blackcurrant bushes swell to more than their normal size before opening, the signs are sinister. This is big bud — the result of the bush being affected by the blackcurrant gall mite. This minute creature carries a virus which will gradually result in a decline in vigour and cropping. Big bud therefore is an indication that the bushes are due for replacement.

Vegetables

34 Protection

Except in very mild areas, crops being overwintered in the ground benefit from some protection. Plants such as parsley, Swiss chard, lettuces and winter radish which are continuing to grow through the winter should be covered with cloches. Those root vegetables, such as carrots, parsnips and beetroot, that are merely being stored in the ground must be treated differently. At the onset of cold weather, pull off the tops, scatter a few slug pellets among the plants and spread straw between and slightly over them, anchoring it in position with a little soil; it is important not to do this until the weather really *is* cold, otherwise the roots will continue to grow beneath the cover, to their ultimate detriment.

35 Tools

Check all garden tools. Tools used for cultivation should always be wiped before they are put away, of course, but should be checked and cleaned now. If any require replacement, remember stainless steel offers enormous advantages in respect of ease of maintenance and durability. Those, such as shears and secateurs, with cutting edges and moving parts must be cleaned (methylated spirits is ideal for removing resin and sap) and oiled: sharpening should be left to an expert. Lawn mowers and other powered tools also benefit from an annual check, if not a complete service, by a qualified service agent: the cost will be repaid by the knowledge that the tool is not only still efficient but also that it is safe.

39 In this mysterious winter landscape few plants would appear to be alive. Yet below the surface, given adequate protection, growth can continue and rhubarb is ripening beneath the terracotta pots.

Vegetables

36 | Supports: gathering

Collect twiggy branches for use as supports for peas and sweet peas – lengths of about 2.5 m (2¾ yd) are the most useful – but do not cut them from trees and hedgerows without first obtaining permission from the owners. In rural areas, a local farmer will often give you permission to collect material when his routine hedging is being done.

37 | Compost bin

Ideally, a proper compost bin should be a cube of about 1.2 m (4 ft) made with slatted sides for good aeration and with the planks on one side removable for ease of loading and unloading. Preferably, it should stand on soil rather than concrete to prevent water-logging. Almost all garden and kitchen organic matter can be composted, avoid chicken carcasses or other animal remains as these can attract vermin; woody matter can be added provided it has first been shredded (a garden shredder makes a very useful and

worthwhile investment). After approximately every 20 cm (8 in) of debris have been added, scatter a proprietary compost accelerator or add a layer of fresh farm or stable manure.

38 | Soil: digging

During mild spells, continue with rough digging, and fork in compost or manure as you do so. No harm is done by digging soil while it is frozen but it is extraordinarily hard work.

39 | Rhubarb: forcing

Force a clump of rhubarb for some tender early sticks by covering it with an old bucket from which the bottom has been knocked out. Even better, and much more attractive, is an old-style terracotta rhubarb pot (several potters now manufacture these to traditional patterns).

40 | Potato tubers: ordering

Around mid season, place orders for seed potato tubers. Unlike seeds, their shelf-life is very limited and only by ordering them ahead of time can you be sure that you will obtain the varieties you prefer, at the right time and of the best quality.

41 | Crops: harvesting

Cut and pull winter lettuce, radishes and other hardy crops as they mature.

42 | Early crops: sowing

In mild areas, at the very end of the season, prepare the ground (see SPRING TASKS **55**) and slow the earliest crops. In cooler regions, wait until early spring, for even if abnormally mild spells occur, the almost certain return of colder conditions will unfortunately render your efforts pointless.

| 37 | If you have space, a double-sided compost bin is ideal. This allows composting to be underway in one section while you fill up the other. The optimum size is a cube of 1.2 m (4 ft). If the bin is any larger composting will be uneven. Add a proprietary compost accelerator or layer of fresh manure approximately every 20 cm (8 in).

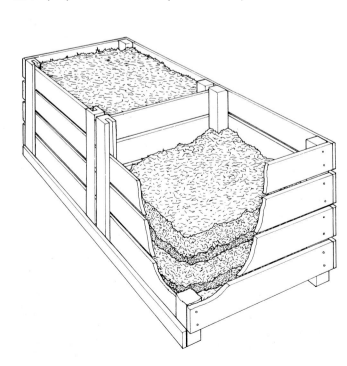

| 39 | A traditional terracotta rhubarb pot is a delightful item in its own right and doubly welcome if it gives you some early sticks of rhubarb. Placed over a clump it forces the rhubarb by excluding the light. You should have tender sticks of fruit in 5 to 6 weeks.

Index

Acknowledgments

The publisher thanks the following photographers and organizations for their kind permission to reproduce the photographs in this book:

8–9 Michelle Garrett/Insight Picture Library; 10 left Christine Ternynck; 10 centre Marijke Heuff (Mr and Mrs Goosenaerts); 10 right Jerry Harpur (Beth Chatto); 11 S&O Mathews; 12–13 Marianne Majerus/Garden Picture Library; 14–5 Christine Ternynck; 18 S&O Mathews; 19 Jerry Harpur (Don Drake)/Elizabeth Whiting & Associates; 21 Eric Crichton; 22 Marijke Heuff (Great Dixter); 23 Jerry Harpur (Heale House); 24 Annette Schreiner; 25 left Jerry Harpur (Barnsley House); 25 right Andrew Lawson; 26 Christine Ternynck; 27 above Christine Ternynck; 27 below Philippe Perdereau; 30 Jerry Harpur (Wisley); 31 left Philippe Perdereau; 31 right Eric Crichton; 32 Michèle Lamontagne; 33 above Michèle Lamontagne; 33 below left Michèle Lamontagne; 33 below right S&O Mathews; 35 Eric Crichton; 38 John Glover; 44 Harry Smith Collection; 46–7 Jerry Harpur (Clare College)/Elizabeth Whiting & Associates; 48–9 Eric Crichton; 51 S&O Mathews; 52 left Gary Rogers; 52–3 Philippe Perdereau; 55 Eric Crichton; 56 Linda Burgess/Insight Picture Library; 57 Jerry Harpur (Mirabel Osler); 58 Gary Rogers/Garden Picture Library; 59 Christine Ternynck; 60 Eric Crichton; 61 Gary Rogers; 62 Jerry Harpur (Ken Akers); 63 Andrew Lawson (Waterperry Gardens); 64 above Georges Lévêque; 64 below Jerry Harpur (Herterton House); 65 above Michèle Lamontagne; 65 below Eric Crichton; 66 and 67 left Jerry Harpur (Johnson)/Elizabeth Whiting & Associates; 67 right Jerry Harpur (Mr Gunn)/Elizabeth Whiting & Associates; 68 Philippe Perdereau; 69 left Eric Crichton; 69 right Jerry Harpur; 70 Michèle Lamontagne; 71 above left Michèle Lamontagne; 71 below Annette Schreiner; 72 Eric Crichton; 73 left Eric Crichton; 73 right Georges Lévêque; 74 Michèle Lamontagne; 75 left Clive Boursnell/Garden Picture Library; 75 right Jerry Harpur (East Lambrook)/Elizabeth Whiting & Associates; 76 Eric Crichton; 77–9 Eric Crichton; 80 above right Sharon Hutton; 80 below left Eric Crichton; 80 right Jacqui Hurst/Boys Syndication; 81 Pat Hunt; 82 Jerry Harpur (Ken Akers); 92 Eric Crichton; 93 Dennis Davis/Garden Picture Library; 94–5 Eric Crichton; 96–7 Michèle Lamontagne; 99 above Jacqui Hurst/Boys Syndication; 99 below Linda Burgess/Insight Picture Library; 100–1 Andrew Lawson; 105 Philippe Perdereau; 106–7 Gary Rogers; 107 right Stefan Buczacki; 109 centre Annette Schreiner; 109 right Philippe Perdereau; 110 Jacqui Hurst/Boys Syndication; 111 left Georges Lévêque; 111 centre Gary Rogers; 111 right Georges Lévêque; 112 above Brian Carter/Garden Picture Library; 112 below Eric Crichton; 113 Eric Crichton; 114 Jacqui Hurst/Boys Syndication; 115 Eric Crichton; 116 Ron Sutherland/Garden Picture Library; 119 Karl Dietrich-Buhler/Elizabeth Whiting & Associates; 124 Eric Crichton; 126–7 Roger Hyam/Garden Picture Library; 132 Christine Ternynck; 133 above left Jerry Harpur (Ken Akers); 133 above right Andrew Lawson; 133 below Heather Angel/Biofotos; 135 Eric Crichton; 136 left Jerry Harpur (Brian Daly and Allan Charman); 136–7 Jerry Harpur (Cranborne Manor); 138 Jerry Harpur (Ken Akers); 139 right Michelle Garrett/Insight Picture Library; 140 Michèle Lamontagne; 141 left Heather Angel/Biofotos; 142 Andrew Lawson; 143 Jerry Harpur (Brian Daly and Allan Charman); 144–5 Christine Ternynck; 146 left Andrew Lawson; 150 Andrew Lawson; 151–153 Stefan Buczacki; 154 Mr Halliday; 155 Stefan Buczacki.

Special photography by Andrew Lawson for Conran Octopus:

Mary Keen's garden 1, 2–3, 4, 6–7, 16–17, 102 left, 108–9 130, 146 right, 148–9, 156.
Cob Stenham's garden 28, 29, 102 right, 103, 129, 139 left and centre, 141 right, 147.

The publishers would particularly like to thank Mary Keen and Cob Stenham for allowing their gardens to be photographed throughout the seasons.